Edward $\heartsuit$ P9-CRF-865

St. Paul Police Dept.

POLICE OPERATIONS

Policies and Procedures

400 FIELD SITUATIONS WITH SOLUTIONS

E. J. STEENBERG
786 LAKEVIEW AV.
ST PAUL, MINN.
55117

POLICE OPERATIONS

Policies and Procedures

400 FIELD SITUATIONS WITH SOLUTIONS

Second Edition

By

JOHN P. KENNEY, Ph.D.

Professor and Director, Institute for Police Studies
Department of Criminology
California State College at Long Beach

and

JOHN B. WILLIAMS, LL.M., M.S. in P.A.

Associate Professor
California State College at Los Angeles

C H A R L E S   C   T H O M A S   ·   P U B L I S H E R
Springfield   ·   Illinois   ·   U.S.A.

Published and Distributed Throughout the World by

CHARLES C THOMAS • PUBLISHER

BANNERSTONE HOUSE

301-327 East Lawrence Avenue, Springfield, Illinois, U.S.A.

NATCHEZ PLANTATION HOUSE

735 North Atlantic Boulevard, Fort Lauderdale, Florida, U.S.A.

This book is protected by copyright. No
part of it may be reproduced in any manner
without written permission from the publisher.

© *1968, by* CHARLES C THOMAS • PUBLISHER

Library of Congress Catalog Card Number: 68-18299

With THOMAS BOOKS *careful attention is given to all details of
manufacturing and design. It is the Publisher's desire to present books
that are satisfactory as to their physical qualities and artistic possibilities
and appropriate for their particular use.* THOMAS BOOKS *will be true
to those laws of quality that assure a good name and good will.*

PREFACE

POLICE OPERATIONS: Policies and Procedures is an operational manual. It has been developed to provide guidelines for the patrol officer, the detective, juvenile, vice and traffic officers in meeting their day-to-day problems. Sections have been designed to assist the Chief of Police and other management personnel with planning, organization and training problems. It was written out of our teaching experience with students in the several universities and colleges in which we have taught and is an attempt to meet some of the problems which to them in their work situations in local police agencies appeared most pressing. Its primary debt must therefore be to those students who have suffered with us in seminars, classes, institutes and projects over the past fifteen years.

It has been our observation that most police agencies have not provided their personnel with adequate directives, orders, and operational information to meet day-to-day problems. Communication of legal and policy information to the field officer is often inadequate and resources by which the officer may be aided in arriving at even a practical solution to many problems is often lacking. Urged by our students, who have been mostly police officers, supervisors and chiefs of police, this volume has been prepared with a view to provide legal, policy and/or practical solutions to the more common management and operational police problems. Some 3,000 procedural problems were identified by the students, from which the 400 included have been selected as covering the majority of police situations. The students have also provided many of the answers which we have given. In addition, we have carefully reviewed time and again with succeeding groups of students many of the problems and their answers to make certain that the practical needs of police agencies could be met by publication of the volume.

Much of the material in the policy and organization sections appeared in varying forms in police management surveys of police agencies, thus being subjected to valuable critique by mayors, councilmen, city managers, newspaper editors, the public, and numerous police officials. These critiques have been invaluable to us in the presentation of the material in its final form.

We are appreciative of all the help we have received, but we assume final responsibility for the contents.

JOHN P. KENNEY
JOHN B. WILLIAMS

CONTENTS

PART V

APPENDIX A

APPENDIX B

APPENDIX C

APPENDIX D

APPENDIX E

POLICE OPERATIONS
Policies and Procedures
400 FIELD SITUATIONS WITH SOLUTIONS

PART I

THE MANUAL AND ITS USE

A POLICE department performs many functions. It enforces laws, it provides a multiplicity of services to the people, it investigates license applicants, fingerprints taxi drivers, and controls crowds, among a host of responsibilities. Because of these many responsibilities policemen are daily confronted with a number of problem situations requiring all kinds of decisions and actions. Each type of activity does not occur regularly for the individual officer and often only once in his career. Training, verbal directives, and occasional written orders do not keep him abreast of all the answers for all the situations. A handy reference guide can provide invaluable assistance. This manual is such a guide both for management and the individual field officer. It is a supplement for an existing manual.

It is suggested that copies of this manual, with loose-leaf binder supplements, be made available to all officers and concerned city officials. When adapted to your department it becomes the principal operational guide for police activities.

The manual contains general guidelines for the operation of any police department. Its contents include a brief review of police and their responsibilities, model organizations and a work schedule which may be adapted to your requirements and policies and procedures. The appendices cover specific information or problem areas common to most police agencies. Supplement this information in a companion loose-leaf binder and you have a completed manual for your department.

The two most important sections of this volume are on policies and procedures. They contain the basic elements essential for effective departmental operations. Adapted to your needs by modifications and supplements, they will provide the basis for most departmental activity. The procedures cover more specifically law enforcement problems. Other procedural areas may be included in the suggested loose-leaf binder supplement.

HOW TO USE THE MANUAL

1. Organization. Compare your existing organization with the model charts which have been reproduced. Adapt yours to the model or reproduce your own chart for inclusion in the loose-leaf binder supplement for ready reference by all officers.

Use the suggested work schedule as a guide for preparation of permanent schedules based on positions in your organization. Adjust working hours to peak periods of departmental activity. Make transfers by *positions* and not on the basis of officers' names.

2. Policies. Basic functional and objective guidelines with some specific policy suggestions have been provided. Policies by definition are general in order to cover a number of similar situations or problems. It will be necessary to identify the specific policy statements which pertain to your operation. These may be underlined in the book for ready reference. Supplemental policies and sub-policies should be prepared and included in the officer's loose-leaf binders. References to policies in the book may be made by page number.

3. Procedures. The procedures section deals with problems most often encountered by the field officer. The answers are in effect "line" procedures. They have purposely been written in general terms and in no way should be construed as the only answers to the problems. To supplement the answers reproduce code sections, policy statements or specific departmental procedures, and cross reference between officers' notebooks and this volume. Your manual section on "line" procedures is then complete.

Since principal emphasis of this manual is on line operations, procedural sections dealing with administrative and auxiliary operations is necessary. These sections should cover such activities as clerical operations, records and communications, property, and personnel. They should be included in the loose-leaf binder.

4. Appendix B is a statement about your city government. Complete the blanks and all officers have immediately available basic information about the city which relates to their position.

5. General and Special Orders. Appendix C outlines a simple method for preparation of orders. They should appear in the loose-leaf binder supplement. Sufficient copies should be made for a distribution to all manual holders.

TRAINING AND SUPERVISION

Training and supervision of police employees may be facilitated by proper use of this manual. The following charts have been designed for use in training the recruit, the continuous training of all officers, and for performance evaluation. If the chart is used continuously, a running record is available showing the officer's ability to perform required duties, and his knowledge about the department and his job. Furthermore, training and supervision becomes an integrated, continuous process, an ideal desired but seldom achieved.

The charts provide a simple method of organizing and recording information about the job and the worker. When properly used, the charts will assist in:

Determining individual and group training needs,

Planning and scheduling training,

Determining the extent to which the supervisor is carrying out his supervisory and training responsibilities,

Determining the progress and effectiveness of training,

Making work assignments.

The following two forms have been designed to provide a permanent record of both supervisor's and the officer's progress in training and performance evaluation. These forms should be reproduced in sufficient quantities for departmental use and on paper which may be inserted in loose-leaf binders or folders.

HOW TO USE THE FORMS

Supervisor's Record (Form 2)

1. *Recruits*—Each time a recruit is instructed in or performs an activity, it will be noted on the form.
2. *Other officers*—Performance may be evaluated or instructions given and indicated on the form.

3. Each time instruction is provided, a need indicated, or a performance evalulated, the supervisor's evaluation will be indicated on both forms.
4. As assignments change, each officer's record (Form 2) will be passed from supervisor to supervisor.

Officer's Record (Form 1)

The supervisor is to write in each officer's form (Form No. 1) the activity in which instruction was given or which was performed and evaluated. This then becomes a permanent personnel record of the officer's accomplishments and his supervisor's evaluations, and is kept by the officer.

Commanding Officer

The commanding officer should regularly inspect both the Supervisor's Record and the Officer's Activity Form. Such inspections reveal supervisorial weaknesses and strengths, as well as facts about the performance of the officer.

POLICE DEPARTMENT

CITY OF_____

OFFICER'S TRAINING AND PERFORMANCE ACTIVITY RECORD

Officer's Name_____

Activity: Performance or Instruction	Date and Supervisor	Activity: Performance or Instruction	Date and Supervisor
Report Writing Case No. 343 / S /	1 June 1960 Sgt. Jones 21 June 1960 Sgt. Smith		

Form 1

POLICE DEPARTMENT

CITY OF_____

Training and Supervision

Supervisor's Record of Officer's Activity

Period:

From _____   Officer_____

To _____

Activity: Performed or Instructed	Date and Supervisor	Activity: Performed or Instructed	Date and Supervisor
Report Writing Case No. 343 / S /	1 June 1960 Sgt. Jones 21 June 1960 Sgt. Smith		

Filed, Personnel   Approved:

Jacket: Date _____   _____
                                                    (Division Comamnder)
By _____
                                                    Date_____

Form 2

Use of the Forms*

The supervisor should consider each officer in regard to each task performed, or his knowledge about a given section or portion of the manual, note the item in the supervisor's record and the officer's activity record form, and indicate the evaluation by use of the following symbols, or other symbols or numbers as desired.

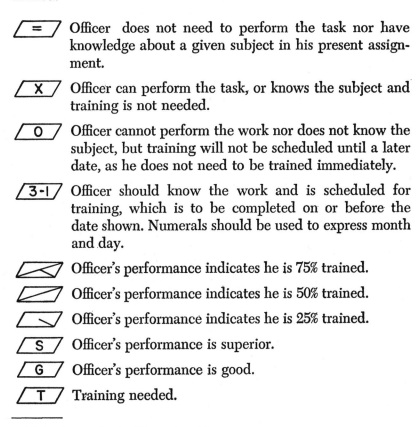

Officer does not need to perform the task nor have knowledge about a given subject in his present assignment.

Officer can perform the task, or knows the subject and training is not needed.

Officer cannot perform the work nor does not know the subject, but training will not be scheduled until a later date, as he does not need to be trained immediately.

Officer should know the work and is scheduled for training, which is to be completed on or before the date shown. Numerals should be used to express month and day.

Officer's performance indicates he is 75% trained.

Officer's performance indicates he is 50% trained.

Officer's performance indicates he is 25% trained.

Officer's performance is superior.

Officer's performance is good.

Training needed.

---

* Reproduce on back of Forms 1 and 2.

PART II

A POLICE CONCEPT

POLICE service is a principal concern of every citizen. It is one of the primary functions of a city, and in incorporating as a city, the citizens desire and obtain local control over their police operation. Such control is accompanied by an obligation to assure effective and efficient police service, particularly in the area of law enforcement, a responsibility delegated to the city upon its incorporation by the state. Other services provided by the police department results from the desires of the citizens, as conceptualized and implemented in ordinances and resolutions by the city council, directives from the city manager or administrator, and by assumption of responsibilities by the police department resulting from requests from citizens.

Good police service does not just happen. It is based on a thorough and comprehensive understanding of what the police job is, how it is to be done, and what it means to the citizens of the community. It is not enough for the police themselves to understand their functions and responsibilities—the citizens and their elected representatives should know. A sampling of citizens, city councilmen, city administrators, and police personnel in several cities reveals that there is not a clear understanding of the role of the police in the community. In order to clarify some of the more fundamental issues, a brief summary of a police concept follows.

The police are the primary civil agency of government responsible for the regulation of conduct and protection of life and property. They are responsible for assuring that orderly activities of society may proceed. Their purposes are to control and/or apprehend those members of society who do not conform, and to assist other duly constituted agencies of government in the creation of an orderly environment. The extent of police activity is circumscribed by laws, court decisions, and customs in the society in which they operate.

15

Objectives of the Police

1. To assure that the orderly activities of the community may
   proceed.
2. To protect life and property against criminal attack.
3. To provide services to the individual members of the society
   and to other governmental units.
4. To prevent crime and delinquency.
5. To endeavor to create an environment of stability and security in the community.

Functions

In order to achieve the objectives set forth for the police, the
following functions are performed:

1. Crime control covers all police activities that have as their
objective control of criminal activity. This function includes enforcement of criminal laws and prescribes the role of the police
in the total picture of the administration of criminal justice.

2. Crime prevention refers to those police activities that have
as their objective the elimination of the desire on the part of
people to commit crime. The ultimate objective of all police
activity is to prevent crime, and in the performance of this
function, the police work closely with other community agencies,
and specifically direct their efforts toward work with juveniles in
order to redirect youthful efforts. The possibilities of police activities in this field are infinite.

3. Control or regulation of conduct includes those police activities that have as their objective enforcement of rules and regulations (prescribed by laws and ordinances, or by the social demands of the community) designed to promote a uniform standard of activity among all people. Such rules and regulations do
not usually carry with them a stigma of criminality.

4. Provisions of services relates to the numerous miscellaneous
activities performed to assist individuals or other units of government, some related to the basic police functions listed above, but
mostly performed as an assumed or directed function of government.

Historical perspective in the United States shows that the police followed the development of the Anglo-Saxon law. The creation of the first uniformed police in England, the London Metropolitan Police Force in 1829, followed a long period of change in the law, from that of severe penalties for even minor violations, to one of moderation and recognition of the need for regularized control over the criminal elements of society. The Metropolitan Police were a culmination of such thinking. Uniformed police in the United States followed shortly therafter, and the concept which influenced the creation of the Metropolitan Police also influenced the beginnings of police in the United States. Probably more important, however, was the tremendous emphasis on the rights of the individual, so much a part of the American society exemplified in the Common Law, the Bill of Rights, and legal decisions down through the history of the United States. These factors influenced the police of this country to emphasize to a great degree the concept of crime prevention, which although warped at times, nevertheless is the philosophical base for police operations.

The service role has been expanded in the last five or six decades. Police are called on regularly to provide miscellaneous information, console the bereaved, deliver babies when medical help is out of reach, help out destitute families, assist stalled motorists, help people unlock doors, and a score of like services. They help other governmental units by delivery of money to the banks for the treasurer, they blockade streets for the department of public works, and they report broken water mains and street lights out, among other services.

It is in the area of prevention and service that it is most difficult to measure the quantity and quality of police services provided. Unfortunately, in most police departments much of the activity in those two areas is not even recorded. The recipients of such service, and the belief by the people in the community that such service is effectively and efficiently being performed is probably the only criteria of measurement, however inexact this may be.

In dealing with the crime problem, the police have a certain amount of tangible evidence of their activity, since a report of police action taken is made. These reports provide a statistical base for indicating the relative amount of criminal activity going on in the community. Such statistical information is not a precise measurement of the amount of crime, nor does it reflect the total number of police actions taken wherein a crime has in fact been committed. Legislation is permissive in that an officer has discretion in the making of an arrest. In a number of minor cases, wherein the officer feels the cause of justice is better served by not arresting a person, no formal action is taken, and often no official report results. Likewise, it is not generally wise to compare the statistics of one community with those of another. Reporting procedures, classification of crimes, and general policies governing police operations condition the statistical information which is available. It is better to compare the record of a department with its previous records of activity.

All crime control activity does not result in the development of cases. In fact, much of a department's personnel time is spent in repressive crime control activities, reflected in patrol by roving surveillance, inspections, and in the gathering and collation of intelligence information on the general problems of crime, the latter being provided through discussions with individuals in the community who are concerned with the protection of the property, or who have knowledge about undesirable behavior patterns of certain citizens.

Traffic control operations are somewhat more amenable to objective evaluation than other police activities. It is feasible to relate enforcement activities to the accident patterns in the community. It is also feasible to evaluate subjectively and quite accurately the effective flow pattern of traffic through the city streets in terms of expeditiousness and safety. Likewise, the results of certain safety educational programs, such as a bicycle safety program, can easily be evaluated in terms of a reduction in the number of children injured.

For an effective police operation, there cannot exist dual standards for the enforcement of criminal law and traffic law in a community. Favoritism cannot be expected or tolerated. Discretion in the interest of justice and in the achievement of departmental objectives is defensible, but there should be like treatment for all individuals irrespective of economic or social status in the community. This imposes a civic responsibility on citizens of a community not to ask for, nor to expect favoritism, and upon the police officers to be as objective as is humanly possible in carrying out their respective responsibilities.

Effective police service results when there is responsiveness to the needs and desires of the people of the community for service. As has been indicated, the police department is not only an agency for crime control and law enforcement, but it is also an important community service agency which the citizens of the community can come to value highly, and from which they should expect prompt and efficient help. However, police service is expensive, and if a police department is to provide more than the accepted basic services, the citizens of a community must recognize that they will have to pay for the services they receive.

The areas of activity in which a local community receives "the extras" of police services would include special traffic safety programs, extra attention to specific traffic problems in a particular area, and special attention at public places of entertainment, parks, school grounds, and playgrounds. However, it must be recognized that there is a real fine line between what are called "extras" and what are basic police service responsibilities. Perhaps the former may best be categorized by the feelings of highly personalized service received by the citizens of a community.

In a metropolitan area, it is incumbent upon all police agencies to cooperate actively with other law enforcement agencies. This is particularly true of those agencies in the suburban areas which must rely on the larger metropolitan police agencies for much information regarding the crime picture in the total area, as well as for assistance in the apprehension of offenders and recovery of property. All suburban police agencies should actively seek the support of the larger counterpart, as well as police agencies in the cities with contiguous boundaries or which are nearby. This is true for both routine police operations as well as in the handling of the emergency situations, but especially in the investigation of criminal cases.

ACTIVITIES

Police activities generally fall into three classes:
1. Cases
2. Field activities
3. Community coordination

Cases provide tangible evidence of police activities. There are criminal cases, traffic cases, and service cases. Usually, all cases will result in some kind of a written record being made by the police department.

Field activities are essentially for the purpose of prevention and repression of crime, regulation of conduct, and to have personnel available to handle cases when, where, and as they occur. They include inspectional services designed to reduce the opportunities for the commission of crime. Inspections are made of business and industrial establishments and situations and incidents which arise in the course of a policeman's duty. The other major component of field activities is that of surveillance. As policemen move around on beats or in assigned areas, they are available to take action in situations requiring it, and it is by this means that they create the impression of "omnipresence," which has the effect of reducing opportunity or belief in opportunity for the commission of crime. In the course of performing inspectional services and in providing surveillance, policemen are available to control and regulate the conduct of people. Between 60 and 70 percent of all police services are field in nature.

The role of the police in *community coordination* is to develop overall crime prevention programs. It is also a means by which the police make available information on crime and other police activities which are of concern to other agencies and to the public at large. The police have a responsibility to work closely with other agencies in developing what may be called a healthy environment, and it is through activities in community coordinating councils and other community organizations that they can be of assistance.

Operations

In order to maintain a complete police service, a police department engages in three broad areas of activity. First are those which have to do with the primary line operations concerned with achieving police objectives. Second are the auxiliary activities required for the performance of the primary police duties, and third are the administrative activities essential for management of the department.

The primary line activities may be broken down into field operations, investigations, and crime prevention. The field operations are essentially those that are undertaken for the purpose of patrol and traffic control. Investigation is concerned with the detective, vice, and juvenile operations. Crime prevention is oriented toward coordination work with community agencies, and activities engaged in by the police, designed to redirect individuals away from criminal activity. The auxiliary activities include records, communications, property, laboratory and equipment control. Administrative activities include operations of the chief of police, personnel, budget, planning, public relations, and reporting activities.

PART III

ORGANIZATION

ORGANIZATION reflects relationships between personnel and units of the department as they are structured to perform the police tasks and duties necessary to achieve departmental objectives. A department's organization can do much to facilitate operations, or it can hamper operations. Each department must develop its own organization to best meet the prevailing conditions of the environment in which it operates. There is no one best organization, but the following charts, schedule, and information may serve to improve or clarify organizational problems.

The charts and accompanying work schedule have been prepared to provide organizational guides for the small and medium sized departments. Limited specialization has been emphasized, based on the premise that more effective police work results from greater deployment of personnel in field and investigation activities. It should be noted that the schedule provides for a full eight hours of work, exclusive of the lunch period for all employees. Overlapping shifts make possible greater concentration of personnel during peak traffic periods and performance of miscellaneous station duties, such as feeding of prisoners or preparation of reports without loss of effective field strength.

Chart II provides for an administrative assistant to the chief of police, who would be responsible for functions similar to those performed by the administration division in Chart III.

Chart III shows an integrated auxiliary service and field operation which affords continuous direct supervision over the station and field personnel.

Both Charts II and III provide for integrated investigation operations, but for some departments, it may be advisable to separate juvenile and adult investigations.

Statements of unit functional responsibilities which appear in

25

Charts IV and V may be prepared for each sub-unit in larger organizations. They have been prepared here principally to serve as a guideline for preparation of a functional organizational chart.

CHART I

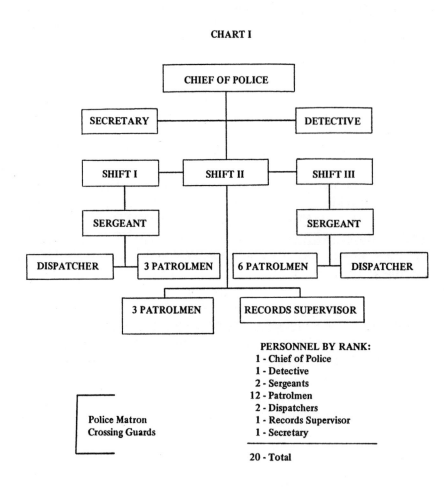

PERSONNEL BY RANK:
1 - Chief of Police
1 - Detective
2 - Sergeants
12 - Patrolmen
2 - Dispatchers
1 - Records Supervisor
1 - Secretary

20 - Total

Police Matron
Crossing Guards

CHART II

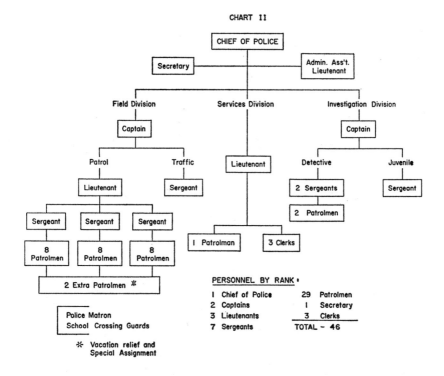

PERSONNEL BY RANK :

1	Chief of Police	29	Patrolmen
2	Captains	1	Secretary
3	Lieutenants	3	Clerks
7	Sergeants	TOTAL — 46	

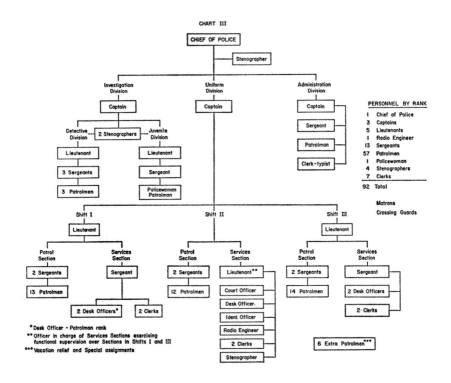

CHART III

CHIEF OF POLICE

Stenographer

| Investigation Division | Uniform Division | Administration Division |

Captain — Captain — Captain

PERSONNEL BY RANK

I	Chief of Police
3	Captains
5	Lieutenants
I	Radio Engineer
13	Sergeants
57	Patrolmen
I	Policewoman
4	Stenographers
7	Clerks
92	Total

Matrons
Crossing Guards

Detective Division — 2 Stenographers — Juvenile Division

Lieutenant   Lieutenant   Sergeant   Patrolman   Clerk-typist

3 Sergeants   Sergeant

3 Patrolmen   Policewoman Patrolman

Shift I   Shift II   Shift III

Lieutenant   Lieutenant

Patrol Section   Services Section   Patrol Section   Services Section   Patrol Section   Services Section

2 Sergeants   Sergeant   2 Sergeants   Lieutenant**   2 Sergeants   Sergeant

13 Patrolmen   12 Patrolmen   Court Officer   14 Patrolmen   2 Desk Officers

              2 Desk Officers*   2 Clerks   Desk Officer.   2· Clerks

                                                Ident. Officer

                                                Radio Engineer

*Desk Officer - Patrolman rank
Officer in charge of Services Sections exercising functional supervision over Sections in Shifts I and III   2 Clerks   6 Extra Patrolmen*
***Vacation relief and Special assignments   Stenographer

CHART IV

FUNCTIONAL ORGANIZATION

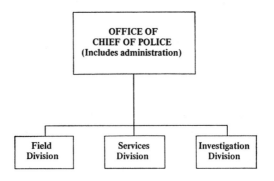

OFFICE OF
CHIEF OF POLICE
(Includes administration)

| Field Division | Services Division | Investigation Division |

CHART V

FUNCTIONAL ORGANIZATION

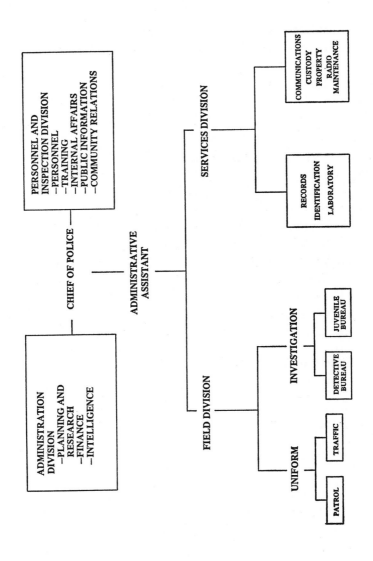

UNIT FUNCTIONS

Office of Chief of Police

1. Be responsible for personnel and training activities.
2. Prepare departmental budget and coordinate its administration.
3. Perform general planning and research functions.
4. Prepare and maintain departmental manual.
5. Be responsible for traffic analytical work and development of traffic control plans.
6. Coordinate purchasing functions for the Police Department.
7. Coordinate vehicular equipment maintenance.
8. Coordinate building maintenance.
9. Research and develop plans to meet specific problems encountered in other divisions.
10. Coordinate the preparation of departmental payroll.
11. Coordinate departmental public relations.
12. Prepare annual report and other administrative reports.
13. Departmental direction.
14. Coordinate departmental intelligence.
15. Be responsible of community relations activities.

Field Division

1. Be responsible for preliminary investigations of all complaints.
2. Make follow-up investigations, as feasible, on all so-called minor cases and major cases which are not specifically assigned to another division.*
3. Answer and make appropriate disposition of all called-for service cases.
4. Regulate citizen conduct and control crowds as required.
5. Make all traffic accident investigations.
6. Be responsible for traffic control, including enforcement of traffic laws.

---

* Minor cases include petty thefts, disturbance of the peace cases, abandoned automobiles, and barking dog cases. Major cases include burglaries, robberies, rapes, murders, forgeries, aggravated assault, and auto theft.

7. Patrol streets and business sections of the city to suppress criminal activity.
8. Assist in emergencies such as fires, floods, and earthquakes.
9. Make inspections of business, industrial, and recreational facilities.
10. Perform other work as required or directed.

Services Division

1. Maintain departmental records; complaint and criminal.
2. Perform clerical and stenographic tasks.
3. Provide communication—radio, telephone, and teletype service.
4. Provide information services to the public at the station.
5. Perform all clerical work relating to services to the municipal and other courts, except that which is routinely handled in the investigation division.
6. Be responsible for supplies and station equipment.
7. Maintain and operate the jail.
8. Maintain warrant file and assign warrants for service within the city, mail for service outside the city, and assign for service in adjoining cities as determined by policy.
9. Provide follow-up control over all active cases.
10. Provide internal departmental identification and laboratory services.
11. Vehicle maintenance.

Investigation Division

1. Assist and advise officers of field division.
2. Make follow-up investigations on all so-called "major" cases. Major cases include burglaries, robberies, murders, checks, and rapes.
3. Maintain relationships with outside law enforcement agencies and make follow-up investigations of cases involving other jurisdictions.
4. Process all juvenile cases after investigations have been made by patrol officers, and assist in investigations as necessary.

5. Be responsible for developing and effecting delinquency prevention responsibilities for the department.
6. Make all specialized investigations, such as forged checks, embezzlements, and frauds.
7. Be responsible for vice and narcotics control.
8. Coordinate and evaluate all "minor" investigations.
9. Perform such other investigative work as may be required.

SUGGESTED WORK SCHEDULE FOR CHART II

I. Administrative Personnel

Position	Hours	Sun.	Mon.	Tue.	Wed.	Thu.	Fri.	Sat.
Chief of Police	8:00 a.m.-5:00 p.m.	X*						X
Lieutenant (Adm. Asst.)	8:00 a.m.-5:00 p.m.	X						X
Captains (2)	8:00 a.m.-5:00 p.m.	X						X
Secretary of Chief	8:00 a.m.-5:00 p.m.	X						X

Services Division

Position	Hours	Sun.	Mon.	Tue.	Wed.	Thu.	Fri.	Sat.
Lieutenant	8:00 a.m.-5:00 p.m.	X						X
Patrolman	6:45 a.m.-3:30 p.m.	X						X
Clerk-Dispatcher No. 1	8:00 a.m.-5:00 p.m.	X						X
Clerk-Dispatcher No. 2	12 Noon -8:45 p.m.						X	X
Clerk-Dispatcher No. 3	3:15 p.m.-12 midnt.	X	X					

II. Investigation Division

Detective Section

Position	Hours	Sun.	Mon.	Tue.	Wed.	Thu.	Fri.	Sat.
Sergeant No. 1	8:00 a.m.-5:00 p.m.	X	X					
Sergeant No. 2	8:00 a.m.-5:00 p.m.			X	X			
Patrolman No. 1	8:00 a.m.-5:00 p.m.	X						X
Patrolman No. 2	*To Be Assigned*							

Juvenile Section

Position	Hours	Sun.	Mon.	Tue.	Wed.	Thu.	Fri.	Sat.
Policewoman-Sergeant	8:00 a.m.-5:00 p.m.	X	X					

III. Field Division

Position	Hours	Sun.	Mon.	Tue.	Wed.	Thu.	Fri.	Sat.
Lieutenant	5:00 p.m.-1:45 a.m.	X	X					
Traffic Sergeant	9:00 a.m.-6:00 p.m.	X						X

Shifts I and III—Extra Officers[1]

Extra Patrolmen—Supplement

Position	Hours	Sun.	Mon.	Tue.	Wed.	Thu.	Fri.	Sat.
X 1	4:15 p.m.-1:00 a.m.						X	X
X 2	7:45 p.m.-4:30 a.m.				X	X		

---

* Days off.
[1] Also used for vacation relief.

Shift I[2]—11:45 p.m.-8:30 a.m.

Position	Hours	Sun.	Mon.	Tue.	Wed.	Thu.	Fri.	Sat.
Sergeant					X	X		
Patrolmen								
A 1		X	X					
A 2				X	X			
A 3							X	X
A 4		X						X
A 5			X	X				
A 6						X	X	
A 7					X	X		
Field Officers, including Sergeant, on duty each day		6	6	6	5	5	6	6

Shift II—6:45 a.m.-3:30 p.m.

Position	Hours	Sun.	Mon.	Tue.	Wed.	Thu.	Fri.	Sat.
Sergeant				X	X			
Patrolmen								
B 1					X	X		
B 2				X	X			
B 3						X	X	
B 4		X						X
B 5						X	X	
B 6				X	X			
Traffic Parking								
7	9:15 a.m.-6:00 p.m.	X	X					
8	9:15 a.m.-6:00 p.m.	X	X					
Field Officers, including Sergeants, on duty each day		6	6	6	6	6	7	8

Shift III—3:15 p.m.-12 Midnight

Position	Hours	Sun.	Mon.	Tue.	Wed.	Thu.	Fri.	Sat.
Sergeant					X	X		
Patrolmen								
C 1							X	X
C 2			X	X				
C 3			X	X				
C 4				X	X			
C 5					X	X		
C 6		X	X					
C 7		X						X
C 8		X						X
Field Officers, including Sergeants, on duty each day		6	6	6	6	7	8	6

[2] One officer to be assigned to inside duty on the desk, "Extra Patrolmen" provide for additional field coverage.

PART IV

POLICIES

THE general will or desires of the people relative to control and regulation of conduct of its citizens in the community has been expressed in the Federal and State Constitutions, the City Charters, and Federal, State, and local laws. Court decisions and directives have modified these documents and laws to conform to the present-day mores of our society. The application to the people of a city is dependent upon interpretation and means of implementation, a responsibility of the city officials.

Administrative policies which pertain to the actual operation of the police department and establish guidelines for its activities are more particularly a responsibility of the city officials. The city council has the responsibility for establishing broad guidelines for all city operations, including the police department. The city manager, if the city has one, is delegated responsibility for administration of all municipal operations by the council, and is thus charged with police operations. Within the police department, the chief of police and his staff officers are responsible for establishing policies and procedures for doing the police job. Thus, there exists within the city three levels of authority, all charged with responsibility for the police operation, but each with a different role. All should work together for the common good of the city.

ROLE OF THE CITY COUNCIL OR COMMISSION

The major responsibility of the city council is to indicate to the city manager in general terms what it expects of the police department. Its general policies are set forth in ordinances and resolutions which govern such matters as personnel, budgeting, and equipment. These affect the police department. Once this has been done, the council should hold the city manager and chief of police responsible for the total operation and success of the department.

37

ROLE OF THE CITY MANAGER

The city manager is the chief executive officer and head of the administrative branch of the city government. Specifically, he is responsible for the supervision and direction of the city, including the police department. This means that the police department has to carry out its operations under the general administrative and management policies laid down by the city manager. Policies governing the policing of the city as developed by the council and the police department are a concern of the city manager and should in general have his approval. It is advisable for the chief of police to develop policies in cooperation with the manager. In addition, the city manager should transmit to the city council matters which need council action relative to the police department, and in turn should transmit to the department the policies of the council.

THE ROLE OF THE CHIEF OF POLICE

The chief of police is responsible for developing policies affecting the internal administration of the department. He should also assume a positive role in the management of departmental operations. In the development of internal operational policies, the chief of police should state clearly the work to be done, who is to do it, and how it is to be done. In addition, he must assume responsibility for organizational and staff policies which aid in the accomplishments of the total police function.

GENERAL POLICIES

1. The police shall enforce, in a reasonable and prudent manner, all Federal, State, and local laws and ordinances relating to the control of crime and regulation of conduct.
2. The police shall treat all persons with dignity and respect and in accordance with the dictates of the federal and state constitutions amplified by judicial decisions as related to individual civil liberties and civil rights.
3. The police shall take such action as may be necessary and operate in such a manner as to assure the citizens of the city that orderly activities of the community may proceed without disruption from criminal and irresponsible elements.

4. The efforts of the police department shall be so directed as to help in the creation of an environment in the community which will prevent the occurrence of asocial and antisocial behavior.
5. The police shall be responsible for the protection of life and property from criminal attack, and in emergency situations when the welfare of the community is threatened.
6. The police shall cooperate with and assist citizens of the community and units of the city, county, state, and federal government with such problems in such situations as customs and traditions dictate, in matters both criminal and non-criminal.
7. The police shall treat all persons equally and with fairness, irrespective of race, ethnic group, creed, or societal status.

DEPARTMENTAL POLICIES

General administrative policies, when adopted, establish the policy framework within which the department operates. Objectives and goals are implicit in such policies. It is necessary for the department to interpret and implement the general policies and it does so by first setting forth departmental administrative policies which prescribe what the department shall do in the performance of the necessary functions. Those functions break down into administration, auxiliary services, and line operations. Naturally, the emphasis is on line operations, which have to do with the performance of essential police services. Administrative and auxiliary services are supporting activities, and their only justification for existing is that they aid and assist the line operation. An outline of the functional activities follows, with a statement of objectives, functions, and some policy guidelines, presented as a model for developing definitive guidelines for the department.

ADMINISTRATIVE SERVICES

Objectives: To provide for effective administration, management, and organization of the department.

Functions

1. Policy making
2. Direction

3. Planning
4. Personnel management
5. Budget
6. Supply

Policy Guidelines

1. All policies shall be consonant with achievement of the objectives of the department.
2. Direction of the department shall be for the purpose of achieving maximum coordination and control.
3. Planning shall be carried on for the purpose of coping effectively with tactical and strategic problems.
4. The department shall endeavor to obtain and maintain the highest caliber of personnel possible.
5. Insofar as is feasible, a performance budgeting program shall be maintained.
6. The highest quality supplies and equipment shall be obtained, consonant with the needs of the department.

AUXILIARY SERVICES

Objectives: To facilitate operation of the line activities.

Functions

1. Records
2. Communications
3. Custody
4. Laboratory services
5. Maintenance of equipment and facilities
6. Identification

Policy Guidelines

1. Records and communications activities shall be integrated and centralized physically and functionally.
2. Reports shall be made of all police actions taken.
3. Records shall serve to control offense classification and completeness of investigation.
4. Records shall be available and shall be used to aid in all police operations.

5. Use of records by departmental personnel shall be controlled to avoid loss or damage to the records.
6. Only bona fide agencies or persons other than departmental personnel shall have access to departmental records for reference purposes.
7. Prompt and efficient processing of all calls to the department shall be made.
8. All persons in custody shall be treated fairly and humanely.
9. Facilities and equipment shall be maintained in good order at all times.
10. Criminalistics work for the department shall be performed by a competent police laboratory, with the department performing only diagnostic preliminary processing.
11. All adults arrested and detained shall be photographed and fingerprinted.

FIELD OPERATIONS

A. Patrol[1]

Objectives

1. To control crime
2. To eliminate actual or suspected opportunity for wrong doing;
3. To regulate conduct
4. To provide services
5. To prevent crime

Functions[2]

1. Roving surveillance
2. Called-for services
3. Inspections

---

[1] The purpose of police patrol is to have policemen in the field to perform essential police duties. It is by means of the uniformed patrol force that the police department provides the principal police services to the public.

[2] Roving surveillance is the means by which the uniformed patrol officer checks on activities on his beat and takes action when it is warranted. During periods of roving surveillance, the patrol officer is available to answer calls for services. Calls for services may result in a criminal case or merely a police action being taken. As a part of routine patrol operations, inspections are regularly made of business and industrial establishments and situations which may require or result in police action.

Policy Guidelines

1. Patrolmen shall act as "eyes and ears" for the police administrator.
2. Patrolmen shall maintain continuous and conspicuous operation.
3. Patrolmen shall constantly be available to supply complete area coverage for accomplishment of the police purpose and to perform tasks so as to effectuate this purpose. This means appropriate action when a crime is committed, and the appropriate processing of all requests for services, whether criminal or non-criminal.
4. Patrolmen shall be responsible for all activities in the field except those which interfere with the performance of regular duties and which are performed by specialists.
5. Patrolmen shall be responsible for complete investigation of all cases, including preservation of evidence and making arrests, except in those cases which interfere with the performance of regular duties and those which require the attention of specialists.
6. One-man patrol automobile operation shall be maintained on a 24-hour basis, except when special assignments require additional personnel strength.
7. Two or more patrolmen shall be assigned to answer all calls for service wherein the nature of the situation is not readily ascertainable, and a danger may possibly exist.
8. Patrolmen shall request assistance when making an arrest or inspecting suspicious situations or circumstances.
9. Inspections shall be made regularly of all business and industrial establishments during hours not regularly occupied.

B. Traffic Control

Objectives: To keep order on the streets and highways and to make their use safe and expeditious.

Functions

1. Enforcement of traffic laws.
2. Control of the flow of automobile and pedestrian traffic through the means of direction.

3. Investigation of traffic accidents.
4. Perform traffic educational and engineering duties as are essential for advancing the objectives of the traffic control program.

Policy Guidelines

1. Patrol officers shall be responsible for enforcement of all moving traffic violations, regulation of the movement of traffic, and investigation of accidents.
2. Planning for traffic control activities shall be a staff function.
3. Parking control activities shall be performed by special assignment.
4. Field procedures will be so designed as to give the impression of officer "omnipresence" for the purpose of accident prevention and traffic control.
5. The principles of selective enforcement and visible patrol shall prevail.
6. All traffic accidents, injury, fatal, and noninjury, shall be investigated.

INVESTIGATION

A. Detective Operations

Objectives

1. To make a critical search for truth and information relative to all criminal and noncriminal cases.
2. To gather facts and data on criminal cases in order to effect their proper dispositions.

Functions

1. Coordinate the processing of all cases.
2. Gather and collate information on criminal activities.
3. Make follow-up or complete investigation of criminal cases.
4. Apprehend violators and recover property.

Policy Guidelines

1. Detectives shall aid and assist patrol officers in making investigations when required.

2. Detectives shall be responsible for the follow-up investigation of all criminal cases which cannot be completed effectively and efficiently by patrol officers.
3. Detectives shall have responsibility for the complete investigation of all criminal cases which require technical attention— such as frauds, forgeries, and extortions.
4. The detectives shall be responsible for gathering and collating information on all criminal activities within the city and those in surrounding areas which may affect the city, and for making it available for departmental-wide use.
5. Detectives shall apprehend offenders and recover property, when such is not accomplished by the patrol officers.
6. Detectives shall assist in the investigation of all complex cases, such as safe burglaries, homicides, and forcible rapes.

B. Vice Control

Objective: To enforce laws concerned with the regulation of gambling, narcotics, liquor, and certain illegal sex activities.

Functions

1. Gather and collate information on vice activities.
2. Coordinate the work of the department with other law enforcement agencies responsible for specific aspects of vice control.
3. Apprehend violators of laws concerning vice activities.

Policy Guidelines

1. Insofar as feasible, absolute repressions of vice conditions shall prevail.
2. Every possible effort shall be made toward identifying persons at "higher levels" of vice operations and in gathering evidence to prove their operations.
3. All officers shall take action in vice cases coming to their attention.
4. Procedures shall be established for the disbursement of undercover funds that will assure secrecy and at the same time protect those who disburse funds.
5. Undercover operators and informants shall be used to gather

evidence of vice operations only under carefully controlled conditions, in conformance with legal requirements, and with the approval of the responsible commanding officer.

6. Continuous coordination and cooperation shall be maintained with other law enforcement agencies responsible for control of vice conditions.

C. Juvenile Control—Crime Prevention[1]

Objective: To aid in the correction of those factors or conditions which predispose or precipitate peoples' activities to asocial or antisocial behavior.

Functions

1. Exercise control over the conduct of juveniles and adults who engage in asocial or antisocial behavior, and over those conditions conducive to such behavior.
2. Process appropriately those juveniles and adults who engage in antisocial or asocial acts, for the purpose of preventing recurrence of such behavior.
3. Coordinate police operations and cooperate with community agencies concerned with the prevention of crime.

Policy Guidelines

1. Officers shall cooperate and coordinate with community agencies for the purpose of preventing crime and delinquency.
2. Juvenile officers shall make follow-up investigations of specified cases involving juveniles in which, at the time of the complaint, a juvenile is presumed to have been involved.
3. Juvenile officers shall assist officers of other units in the investigation of cases involving juveniles.
4. Juvenile officers shall make necessary diagnostic background investigation of juveniles involved in cases in order to objectively make appropriate dispositions.
5. Juvenile officers shall make final disposition of all juveniles apprehended or otherwise involved in cases.

---

[1] Police activity in crime prevention has traditionally been directed toward juveniles, but opportunities in this field are infinite.

PART V

GENERAL PROBLEMS

1. An officer receives a complaint that a woman who has two children is living with another woman as "husband and wife."

The officer should proceed to verify the truth of the complaint then proceed to the office of the prosecuting attorney for his recommendations. It is possible that the prosecuting attorney could construe such action as being a violation of some state laws regulating public decency—Lesbianism.

2. A citizen is walking down the sidewalk and comes across a sprinkler which is blocking his path because it is sprinkling across the sidewalk. He kicks it aside and it breaks. The owner complains to you.

Some cities and counties have ordinances which make it a misdemeanor to set a sprinkler so that the water would wet any person walking on the sidewalk. If so, the owner of the sprinkler may be arrested by any witness to the action. On the other hand, a person who maliciously injures the property of another is guilty of malicious mischief.

Under "malicious mischief," the word malicious means an intent to do a wrongful act. In this situation, it would seem that when the person kicked it aside he did not do so maliciously but only to get the sprinkler out of the way. Therefore, there would be no violation. It would seem that the owner of the sprinkler is the one at fault.

3. A desk officer receives a telephone call from a person stating that he has just received a telephone call from his brother in another city, threatening to commit suicide.

In this situation, time is of the essence, hence the complainant should be told immediately to place a long distance call directly to the police department of that city. The police in the city concerned will need the name, phone number, and address of the brother, plus facts as to why he thinks there is a possibility of a suicide. In such cases, it is the duty of all police officers to prevent a suicide, even though in some states suicide is a legal act. If the person calling appears unduly excited, the desk officer should obtain sufficient information which could then be relayed to the police department concerned by the desk officer.

4. An officer is assigned to strike duty where picketing is in progress.

Since a peace officer represents all persons, every peace officer must remain impartial to both management and labor. Strikes are often accompanied

49

with some mass emotions, hence officers should be mentally prepared to disregard verbal abuses, such as razzing and cursing on the part of the strikers or other persons.

Officers should not patrol on company property or use company washrooms. On the other hand, officers should not accept coffee, doughnuts or sandwiches from the strikers. In short, officers should not accept anything from either labor or management.

If an arrest is necessary, it would seem advisable to secure as much assistance as is necessary before taking action. Generally, a verbal warning will suffice, and another course of action would be to secure facts for the issuance of a warrant of arrest at a more opportune time.

5. At the scene of a major fire an officer calls for equipment to block off the area.

Prompt action in such cases may save life and property. Sometimes sightseers flock to such scenes, compound the traffic congestion and hamper the efforts of firemen. Such persons are guilty of a misdemeanor in California under Penal Code Section 409.5 which states: "Whenever a menace to the public health or safety is created by a calamity such as flood, storm, fire, earthquake, explosion, accident or other disaster, officers of the California Highway Patrol, police departments, or sheriff's office may close the area where the menace exists for the duration thereof by means of ropes, markers or guards to any and all persons not authorized by such officer to enter or remain within the closed area. Any person not authorized willfully entering the area or willfully remaining within the area after notice to evacuate shall be guilty of a misdemeanor. Nothing in this section shall prevent a duly authorized representative of any news service, newspaper, or radio or television station or network from entering the area closed pursuant to this section."

6. An officer is patrolling and as he approaches a group of men on the sidewalk, one of the men challenges the officer to fight.

Such an action is a misdemeanor under most state laws relating to disturbing the peace. The officer should question the challenger as to his reason for his action. If no satisfactory reason is given, the offender should be placed under arrest for disturbing the peace. If a satisfactory reason is given (such as "in jest"), the officer should make a field interrogation or interview card and continue his patrol. If an immediate arrest would jeopardize the safety of the officer, he should leave the scene and secure the assistance of other officers before taking any action. Under no circumstances should he accept the challenge.

7. In response to a call, officers are shown an empty iodine bottle by a woman's husband who states that his wife swallowed the contents and locked herself in the bathroom.

First, an ambulance should be requested. Then the officer should attempt to render assistance to the woman. If the woman won't open the door, a forced entry would be in order. The aid rendered would depend upon the amount of training the officer has received in first aid. Sometimes the officer may be able to obtain information by telephone from the hospital as to what action to take or which antidote to give, pending the arrival of the ambulance. After the woman's safety has been assured, some additional police action may be necessary, such as making a written report of the incident, or an arrest and booking if some law has been violated.

8. Due to the tremendous increase in crime in a particular area it is determined to conduct a road blockade to check on all persons leaving or entering the area.

It is generally held by the courts that *indiscriminate* "police blockades," that is, blocking off designated areas and stopping all persons and automobiles entering or leaving such areas and searching them without first obtaining search warrants, are illegal as being "unreasonable" under the provisions of the United States Constitution, Amendment IV.

But "discriminate" road blockades are still legal and *should* be part of good police planning. Situations calling for this type of police action would include blocking off an area where a perpetrator of a major crime has just entered or a homicidal offender is present or a maniac is at large. The type of crime and the vicious propensities of the person will dictate when to activate a police blockade.

9. Upon responding to an assault call an officer is met by the victim of a battery who demands that the assailant be arrested immediately. The misdemeanor had been committed the day before.

Generally, a person may be arrested by another person, or officer, for a misdemeanor committed or attempted in his presence. But this right to make a physical arrest is lost when not made within a reasonable time after its commission. Most courts hold that the lapse of a day is an unreasonable length of time. This does not mean that the victim is without any authority to take action in a criminal prosecution, because he may apply for the issuance of a warrant for the arrest of the assailant. The victim should be so informed and directed to the office of the Prosecuting Attorney to sign the necessary papers.

10. In responding to a fire call an officer finds that a property owner purposely set fire to an old building on his land which is not covered by insurance.

First, the Fire Department should be immediately notified of the situation to prevent the fire from spreading. It should be determined whether or not the owner has any legal authorization from local or county fire officials permitting the fire. If the person has a permit, ascertain that all required safety measures are being taken. If the property owner has no authorization, he should be arrested under the appropriate penal section, such as Arson (a felony) or Unlawful Burning (a misdemeanor or a felony, depending upon the particular State's laws).

11. A mother complains to an officer that her twelve-year-old son was maliciously struck by an adult neighbor.

The first step is to determine the validity of the complaint. After having listened to the mother, and the witnesses (if any), the suspect and the victim should be interrogated separately. It has been found advantageous to question the child out of the presence of his mother because of the possibility of his assenting to whatever his mother says. Next, the suspect should be interviewed.

Experience has shown that many instances of similar nature are a result of neighborhood "grudge" situations. This is not to infer that the complaint is not valid, but it is a consideration in deciding whether criminal action should be instituted by way of an arrest (by the officer if a felony, or by a private person such as the victim) or the taking of a crime report for follow-up action by the officer handling complaints involving juveniles.

12. A person complains to an officer that he was charged too much interest on a loan. The interest rate was 10 percent.

Charging a usurious rate of interest is a crime, but the charge of 10 percent does not usually constitute usury. Some contracts, however, are so worded that only an attorney with a calculating machine may be able to determine the rate of interest. In such cases, the interviewing officer may elect to (1) make a written report, reciting all the facts and pertinent sections of the contract, and have the victim sign, or (2) refer the victim to the office of the prosecuting attorney, where the victim may present his complaint for the possible issuance of a warrant for arrest.

13. An off-duty police officer, unarmed, witnesses a robbery in progress in a supermarket.

Appropriate police action should be taken. Generally, this means that the officer should attempt to subdue and physically arrest the robber. But if the latter is armed, the officer should not take any action which might cause the robber to shoot and thus endanger the life or lives of other persons present. Instead, the officer could mentally record an accurate description of the robber(s), the license number of the automobile, etc., and immediately telephone headquarters for a radiobroadcast.

14. A man approaches an officer on his beat and informs him that he had made a report of his wallet being stolen a month ago and now he had

just seen the pickpocket get on a bus which is already two blocks down the street.

Stealing from the person of another is generally considered to be grand theft which is a felony, and for which an arrest can be made at anytime and place. However, the immediate problem is to overtake the bus, which may be accomplished by securing a police car or the victim's car. Where neither is immediately available, it may be possible to use a taxi. In any event, the victim should accompany the officer for positive identification of the suspect.

15. A detective assigned to tail a suspect sees that another person, unknown to the detective, is also tailing the same suspect.

The investigator should consider the possibilities that the unknown person may be (1) a friend of the suspect; (2) a hired protector or bodyguard; (3) a private detective, or (4) another detective from another or the same police agency. Discretion will probably dictate that the detective should not reveal his presence. Upon returning to headquarters, he can check the possibilities of another having been assigned to the case, and if so, he can make some arrangements for mutual cooperation.

16. An officer in serving a warrant of arrest for a parking violation is informed that the owner sold the vehicle several weeks before the warrant was issued. No proof of sale is immediately available.

If the officer is convinced that the story is true, the warrant should not be served. The person named in the warrant should be directed to appear the next day in the court, which issued the warrant, to establish the prior transfer of ownership or to sign an affidavit that the vehicle had been sold and to whom. The warrant can then be recalled by the court.

If the officer is convinced that the person is an obvious deadbeat, and is merely stalling for time, the warrant should be served in the usual manner. In most cases, this will consist of taking the person to a clerk or other person authorized to receive bail and the return of the person to his home. Where bail is not posted, the person is booked in jail.

17. At the scene of a fire an officer finds that the fire has been extinguished and that no call was made to the Fire Department.

The officer should notify the Fire Department by telephone of the circumstances. If the officer's investigation discloses the possibility that the crime of arson had been committed, the officer should so notify the Fire Department and the personnel assigned for investigation of arson crimes. Pending the arrival of the arson investigator, the officer must protect the suspected crime scene and any evidence collected in connection therewith. This should be followed by a complete and detailed written report.

18. An officer receives an "all units" call to proceed to the scene of a crime.

The quadrant plan for covering a crime in progress may be utilized in the following manner:

The officer on whose beat the crime occurs should proceed to the scene and one or more additional officers should be assigned to assist him. Such other officers as are available should be assigned to a section or sections of the quadrant and begin to patrol in the outer area, working toward the scene in order to block escape routes of the criminal and make an arrest. The quadrant plan may be effected in any location, the center of the cross denoting the crime scene.

THE QUADRANT PLAN

1	2
3	4

In short, the crime scene would be where the lines intersect. Units would proceed to the area from different directions, that is, one unit would approach from area 4, another from the direction 1, and so forth. In this manner, more coverage is afforded, and the chances of escape by a criminal is lessened.

19. As an officer approaches a car parked on a back road, the car pulls away and the occupants throw something into the weeds at the side of the road.

These facts seem to indicate that the officer should stop the car and make inquiry as to the reason for the presence of the occupants of the car in that location. Also, inquiry should be made as to what was thrown away, and they should be detained until the area has been checked for the discarded object. This may be a case of narcotic users, beer drinkers, or mere litterbugs. In any event, the officer should make a thorough check of the occupants and the area before they are released.

20. A person appears at a police station and wishes to report an incident which is usually handled by an officer who is not at the time on duty.

The desk officer should determine if a report should be taken. If he decides that the incident warrants a report, he should complete the appropriate form and have the reporting person sign it. When the taking of the report is beyond the ability or authority of the desk officer, he should refer the person to the proper investigating unit. If the concerned unit is not available, the person should be taken to the watch commander for discussion and decision.

21. An indignant citizen complains that he has just discovered that his house is "bugged."

The unauthorized installation of a Dictograph℗ or Dictaphone℗ in the home of another may constitute a crime. If so, an appropriate crime report should be taken and the microphone, wires, and other equipment should be booked as evidence. In some states, such installations may be legally authorized by the head of the police agency or by a court. In the latter event, a written report should be taken from the complainant, the equipment seized, and eventually, returned to the agency or unit concerned.

22. On night patrol, an officer observes a person pushing lighted papers under a house.

The responsible person may be a psychopathic "fire bug," but in any event, the person should be placed under arrest for arson, unless he has some legal excuse for his action. The officer should put out the fire or call the fire department. He should also save some of the burned paper as evidence.

23. An officer on stakeout near a high school observes two girls in a car force a young boy to enter the car against his wishes.

All parties should be detained for investigation. Since girls are involved, it may be advisable to have a policewoman called to interrogate them, or the girls could be taken to the station for questioning. In any event, it would seem that there is a possibility of a kidnapping being involved, which is a felony. A complete investigation should be made, and a crime report obtained from the boy unless the parties were playing a game or a prank.

24. An officer on patrol in an unpopulated area observes a person walking up a fire road carrying a gun.

The person should be checked for a possible tie-in with some crime report and the serial number of the gun could be checked for possible stolen property. A field interrogation card should be made, and if the person is not violating any trespassing laws, he should be released, if he is also not violating any gun laws.

25. An officer off duty returning home from the night watch, about 2:00 a.m., sees a car parked with two men in it, and notices a flickering light in a hardware store just in front of where the car is parked.

The odds in this case are that a burglary is in progress, hence the officer should proceed as quickly as possible to a telephone and call for assistance. He could instruct the dispatcher to have a car or cars meet him at a designated place out of sight of the parked car so that the officers could formulate a plan of approach and apprehension. Thereafter, the persons could be taken into custody and questioned regarding the highly suspicious circumstances. It would be unusual, and not advisable, for an officer to attempt to handle the situation by himself.

26. A person living near a park complains that a person in a blue sedan, license No. JAV 159, has been taking leaf mold from the park.

Most cities and counties have ordinances covering the unauthorized removal of material from parks. In such situations, the officer should trace the owner of the vehicle through the license number, and may proceed to obtain a warrant of arrest. A report should be made and filed.

27. A person receiving a traffic citation for crossing a double line offers the officer $10.00 to forget it.

Such action constitutes bribery, which provides under most state laws:
"Every person who gives or offers any bribe to any executive officer of this state, with intent to influence him in respect to any act, decision, vote, opinion, or other proceeding as such officer is punishable by imprisonment in the state prison not less than one nor more than fourteen years, and is disqualified from holding any office in the state." The person should be placed under arrest for the above, a felony, the $10.00 booked as evidence, and appropriate reports should be made. Do not forget to write the citation.

28. A tenant in an apartment building complains that her room is "bugged." She has found a microphone under her dining room table. She is recently divorced.

In this situation, the investigating officer should follow the wire connected to the microphone to see if it leads to a connection or a tape recorder. If a recorder is found, it may be advisable to arrange for a stakeout. If all that is found is the microphone, it should be booked as evidence. A crime report should be taken for violation of appropriate state laws and a complete investigation made.

29. At the scene of a felonious assault, the victim tells the officers that he doesn't want any medical attention, and he refuses to give any information regarding his assailant.

When at the scene of any serious injury, officers should immediately summon an ambulance. If after the arrival of the ambulance the victim refuses medical attention, which he has a right to do, officers should take the names of the ambulance attendants and make appropriate written reports regarding the incident. At this point the officers should be careful to ascertain whether or not the victim has such possession of his faculties that it can be said that the latter acted in a rational manner. Putting it otherwise, if the officers believe that the victim is not capable of caring for himself, the victim should be placed in an ambulance and transported to the hospital, because it is one of the duties of an officer to save lives.

As to the assailant, if he is ascertainable he should be apprehended and booked for felonious assault or for assault with intent to commit murder. In this event, appropriate crime and arrest reports should be made.

30. A woman complains to an officer that when she arrives home late at night a man in a car follows her from the streetcar to her apartment.

This could be a violation of disturbing the peace. All "mashers" come within this law. Advise the victim as to her rights to make a citizen's arrest. Officers can arrange to stake out in the vicinity at the time when the offense usually occurs. If this is not feasible, the victim should be instructed to obtain the license number of the car, and appropriate follow-up action or investigation could be made from that information.

31. A person complains to an officer that some unknown person wrote on his car with paint remover.

This is a misdemeanor and is usually designated as malicious mischief. The officer should take a written report and ask for names of possible suspects. The officer should then check the area for the possibility of roving gangs, or an angry neighbor. A search should be made for a discarded bottle or can, which if found, should be checked out for fingerprints or for tracing it to the possible place of original purchase.

32. An officer observes a man at night climbing through a bedroom window into a darkened residence. The man states that he forgot his key, the house is locked, and nobody is home.

The officer should attempt to establish the veracity of his statement by (1) contacting neighbors for identification, (2) asking this man to describe the contents of the room, then verifying same, and (3) questioning him regarding the exact address, telephone number, etc. If the person's story cannot be verified satisfactorily, he should be taken to the station for further checking.

33. An officer is informed by a citizen that a person dumped some trash on his property.

Officers investigating complaints of illegal dumping should refer the complainant to the Office of the Prosecuting Attorney, if the situation does not require immediate police action. The complainant should be advised to obtain the following information: (1) license number and description of the vehicle involved; (2) name, address, and description of the violator; (3) date, time and location of the violation; (4) names and addresses of other witnesses. A written report should be made of the incident. If the officers observe a dumping violation, two possible actions could be taken: (1) Proceed by application for complaint to the prosecuting attorney for violation of the city or county dumping ordinance or of the state law. (2) Make a physical arrest after first obtaining a signed crime report from the owner or person legally in charge of the property. The gist of this offense is that the owner did not give anyone permission to dump debris on his property.

34. A person complains that while she went shopping for dinner the landlord put a padlock on her door. She pays by the month and is one week delinquent in making the monthly payment.

It is the general rule that an officer should not become involved in civil disputes, nor to advise on matters involving civil litigation. However, there is a possibility that this type of action could amount to forcible detainer under some penal statutes. One such statute reads: "Every person using or procuring, encouraging or assisting another to use any force or violence in entering upon or detaining any lands or other possessions of another, except in the cases and in the manner allowed by law, is guilty of a misdemeanor." If it is not clear that there is a violation of the law the complaining party should be referred to the office of the prosecuting attorney for appropriate action. This procedure is not generally very satisfactory to the person involved, but it is the only legal procedure that an officer can follow when there is doubt as to the civil-legal rights of the parties involved.

35. A woman living in an apartment changes the lock on her door, the manager demands a key for this lock so he can inspect the premises at his convenience.

This is approximately the same situation in essence as question No. 34 in that officers are neither obligated nor authorized to disseminate civil advice. Both parties should be referred to an attorney or to the prosecuting attorney for advice in the matter.

36. A beat officer stops a suspect, and upon checking his record, determines that the suspect is an unregistered ex-convict.

The United States Supreme Court has ruled that the ex-convict registration law of the city of Los Angeles, California, is unenforcible, unless the officer first notifies the person that he has to register, or, unless the ex-convict has knowledge that he should have registered. In the latter situation, the ex-convict should be arrested forthwith, but if there is any doubt as to whether or not he had knowledge that he should have registered, the officer should make an appropriate field interrogation card of the incident for follow-up investigation by the detectives. If the ex-convict requests that he be allowed to register immediately, it would probably be a good idea to take him to the department for registration and further check out.

37. An officer stops a person for a field interrogation, but the person runs. After catching him the suspect is unable to speak English.

The officer should find an interpreter to question the suspect. Although a failure to speak English is a circumstance which should cause the officer to suspect that there may be a violation of the immigration laws, there are many thousands of people in the United States who do not speak English. Therefore, an arrest for violation of immigration laws should not be made solely upon this circumstance alone. A thorough investigation seems to be in order because of the general rule that innocent people do not run and that running from an officer is evidence of guilt of some crime. Mere running from an officer will not justify shooting by the officer. There must be other evidence that the person is connected with some felony.

38. On a routine bar inspection a patrolman finds two citizens making amends after an obvious fight. One of the men is badly cut by an apparent knife wound. No one involved wishes to make a complaint.

A bad cut is a felony under most state laws which read: "Every person who commits an assault upon the person of another with a deadly weapon or instrument or by any means of force likely to produce great bodily injury is punishable by imprisonment in the state prison not exceeding ten years, or in a county jail not exceeding one year, or by fine not exceeding five thousand dollars, or by both such fine and imprisonment."

Under this section it is possible to arrest a suspect, if identifiable, even though a victim may not wish to prosecute. This is sometimes done when there is some danger of death resulting from the cut. If such action is taken the officer should make out the arrest report and crime report, signing both, and include a statement to the effect that the victim did not wish to prosecute nor sign a crime report.

The arrest if made in this situation is because a crime is against the "people of a state" rather than against an individual and the officer represents "the people."

39. Gasoline and oil are spilled on the street.

Generally, such action is accidental rather than intentional, in which case the officers should call the Fire Department to wash the gasoline and oil off the street in order to reduce the hazard to traffic. Some departments radio such information to their motorcycle officers as a precautionary measure to prevent the officers from driving through such a dangerous portion of the road. Deliberate spilling would call for police action with a physical arrest or application for complaint. (See case 40.)

40. An officer observes a dangerous condition existing in the street.

If a hazardous condition is observed which endangers life or property, or which might create a civil liability to the city, the scenes should be isolated by utilizing barricades. Requests for emergency street service and/or barricades should be made for the following hazards: (1) damaged streets and sidewalks; (2) broken guard-rails; (3) oil spills, glass, and other debris constituting a hazard in the street; (4) landslides on the street; (5) fallen trees on the street; (6) any other hazard on the street which might create a civil liability to the city, and (7) other hazards which might be dangerous to life. Pending the arrival of the barricades, the officer should set out flares and stand by to protect the scene as much as possible.

41. An officer receives an "unknown trouble" call, and upon arrival finds the door open. There is no sound nor activity.

Discretion indicates that the officer should proceed with caution, being alert and ready for any kind of an emergency. A plan of approach should be decided upon by the officer or officers before an entry is made so that there would be no danger of one officer mistaking another for a suspect in the dark. Different approaches are made for small residences and large buildings in commercial areas, so that no real information can be spelled out which would be applicable to all situations. Each situation presents different problems.

42. A beat officer is confronted by a citizen who points out another citizen who has just littered the sidewalk.

Since this was a misdemeanor not committed in the presence of the officer, the arrest should be made by the complainant. If the littering was made on a street, then another type of violation may have occurred. If there is a county or city ordinance, then an arrest should be made under it.

43. A beat officer is confronted by a citizen who points out another citizen who has just put a slug in the telephone.

Since the officer did not witness the misdemeanor committed, the arrest should be made by the complainant. However, the officer should first call the telephone company to find out if they wish to prosecute and be guided accordingly, since the phone company would be the victim.

44. An officer on patrol is stopped by a public park attendant who states there is a woman in the park who is washing her clothing in a drinking fountain.

If there is a city or county ordinance prohibiting such action, an arrest could be made. If not, the woman should be warned against such activity and advised to cease her actions because her action may possibly amount to a disturbing of the peace as not being conducive to the public welfare or health.

45. An officer on patrol observes a man walking out of a public park carrying a live duck. The park contains several ducks of a similar variety.

There are several possibilities prevailing in this situation:
1. Possible petty theft, a misdemeanor.

2. Possible receiving of stolen property, a felony.
3. Possible drunk, a violation under the appropriate city or county ordinance, or state law.
4. It may be his duck, which he is taking for a walk.

The officer should conduct an investigation as to whether or not any of the above, or other, conditions exist before taking action.

46. An officer on an emergency robbery call almost collides with an obviously drunk driver, who has just run a red light.

Generally, the officer should continue to answer the robbery call. If he does so, he should radio communications regarding the drunk driver, so another police car can be dispatched to handle the case. Sometimes the officer can inquire of communications if another car is closer to the robbery, in which case the other car could be assigned to answer the robbery call, and the first officer could arrest the drunk driver. At this point, however, it should not be overlooked that the drunk driver may be making good his escape after having committed the robbery.

47. A manager of a theater informs an officer that he has just received an anonymous telephone call that a time bomb would explode in the theater in half an hour. There are about 500 persons in the theater.

The officer has no legal right under most state laws to order evacuation of the premises. Hence it should be explained to the manager that it is his decision as to whether or not he wishes the officer to announce that the place should be evacuated. While the manager is making up his mind, the officer should obtain a bomb expert and notify the fire department. If an evacuation is decided upon by the manager, the officer should call for assistance and obtain other officers to help with the crowd, traffic congestion, and perhaps have an ambulance at the scene. The explosives detail should be given assistance in making a complete search of the premises. Under some laws it is a felony to make a false bomb report, therefore a thorough investigation should be made.

48. An officer is stopped by a citizen who tells him that a woman is about to jump off a ten story building two blocks away.

Even though in some states suicide is a legal act, the officer is under a duty to preserve life and property. Consequently, the officer should immediately proceed to the scene and call for assistance. The assisting officers could block off the area into which the woman might possibly jump while other officers should proceed to the place where the woman is and make every effort to prevent her jumping. Officers have been successful in these situations in securing the assistance of doctors or clergymen or some other interested person. In any event, a cautious approach and an understanding manner will do much to distract the person so that the person may be seized.

49. An officer is called to a park where a citizen complains about the large crowd gathered to listen to speeches on Communism.

Speeches on Communism are generally legal and officers should not make any attempt to interfere with free speech. However, some speeches may amount to "criminal syndicalism." Most state laws describe criminal syndicalism as follows:

"The term criminal syndicalism as used in this act is hereby defined as any doctrine or precept advocating, teaching, or aiding and abetting the commission of crime, sabotage (which word is hereby used as meaning wilfull and malicious physical damage or injury to physical property), or unlawful acts of force and violence or unlawful methods of terrorism as a means of accomplishing a change in industrial ownership or control, or affecting any political change.

Any person who:

1. By spoken or written words or personal conduct advocates, teaches, or aids and abets criminal syndicalism or the duty, necessity or propriety of committing crime, sabotage, violence or any unlawful method of terrorism as a means of accomplishing a change in industrial ownership or control, or affecting a political change; or,

2. Wilfully and deliberately by spoken or written words justifies or attempts to justify criminal syndicalism or the commission or attempt to commit crime, sabotage, violence or unlawful methods of terrorism with intent to approve, advocate, or further the doctrine of criminal syndicalism; or,

3. Prints, publishes, edits, issues or circulates or publicly displays any book, paper, pamphlet, document, poster or written or printed matter in any other form, containing or carrying written or printed advocacy, teaching, or aid and abetment of, or advising, criminal syndicalism; or,

4. Organizes or assists in organizing, or is or knowingly becomes a member of any organization, society, group or assemblage of persons organized or assembled to advocate, teach or aid and abet criminal syndicalism; or,

5. Wilfully by personal act or conduct, practices or commits any act advised, advocated, taught or aided and abetted by the doctrine or precept of criminal syndicalism, with intent to accomplish a change in industrial ownership or control, or affecting any political change; is guilty of a felony and punishable by imprisonment in the state prison not less than one nor more than fourteen years." Such incidents are usually recurrent, which gives the officer sufficient time to consult with a prosecuting attorney before an arrest is made.

50. An officer receives a "woman screaming and possible homicide" call, and upon arrival hears screaming. Upon demanding admittance, a man opens the door about two inches and upon seeing the officer he slams the door shut. The officer concludes that a felony may be in progress and

proceeds to break in the door. It turns out that it is merely a loud radio program and that the man is drunk.

Officers are authorized to arrest in cases where they have reasonable cause to believe a felony is being or has been committed. Most state laws provide: "To make an arrest, a private person, if the offense be a felony, and in all cases a peace officer, may break open the door or window of the house in which the person to be arrested is, or in which they have reasonable grounds for believing him to be, after having demanded admittance and explained the purpose for which admittance is desired." This means that under the circumstances presented in this case, it would seem that the officer took a lawful but erroneous course of action. Since the action was lawful, the officer acted properly. A written report should be made of all the facts and circumstances concerning the event.

51. A woman complains that her boy friend borrowed her car a week ago and she hasn't seen him since. She wants to make a stolen car report.

It is possible that such action constitutes grand theft auto, either a felony or a misdemeanor. The difference between the two crimes will depend, in this situation, upon the intent of the taker or upon the agreed purpose for which the car was to be used. If there is a conclusion that intent to steal has been shown, a stolen car report for grand theft auto would seem appropriate. It should be explained to the complainant that she will be expected to testify in court against her boy friend.

52. An officer observes four boys in their late teens placing a heavy steel bar across a railroad track used by passenger trains. The boys break and run when he approaches.

The adage "first things first" would direct the officer to remove the obstruction, and then use every means to capture the wrongdoers. After this, the officer should make a report to the railroad company involved and a written report for departmental records. If the boys are arrested, they should be booked for attempted train wrecking, which is covered in most state laws as follows:

"Every person who unlawfully throws out a switch, removes a rail, or places any obstruction on any railroad with the intention of derailing any passenger, freight or other train, car or engine, or who unlawfully places any dynamite or other explosive material or any other obstruction upon or near the track of any railroad with the intention of blowing up or derailing any such train, car or engine, or who unlawfully sets fire to any railroad bridge or trestle, over which any such train, car or engine must pass with the intention of wrecking such train, car, or engine, is guilty of a felony and shall be punished by imprisonment in the state prison without possibility of parole."

53. An officer, in the night-time, discovers a freshly broken window at the rear of a business establishment in the downtown area.

The officers should immediately inform headquarters regarding this situation. From this point on two courses of action are suggested: (1) notify the owner of the business so that he may come down and secure the broken window; pending his arrival the officer should protect the property, or (2) the officer could arrange for a stakeout in the event that some person might return to make an entry. In such a case the owner should be contacted and advised that he should not come down until the stakeout has been completed.

The above presupposes of course that the officer has first obtained sufficient assistance to make a thorough check of the premises to verify the presence or absence of a burglar inside.

54. An officer on routine patrol observes an unsaddled horse wandering about a residential neighborhood late at night.

Horses or other animals roaming around at large should be taken into protective custody and released to the owner. This is done by obtaining a rope or clothesline and leading the horse back to the station or possibly turning the horse over to the local pound or humane society. Since this is occurring late at night, it would not seem practical to awaken the neighbors to inquire as to the ownership of the animal. Instead, it would seem practical to have the day officer canvass the area for possible information as to where the animal belongs.

55. The officer working the release desk at the jail (where prisoners who have served their time are released, and bailouts, etc., are released), in checking his prisoners' records, finds that one who should have been released a week ago is still in custody.

The officer should notify his superior immediately, and the office of the prosecuting attorney. The latter will usually make suggestions which should be followed. In any event, the prisoner should be released immediately, and written reports regarding the error should be made. The person responsible for the error should also be notified and directed to file appropriate reports.

56. The custodian of the jail is in charge of the trustees. Two of the trustees get in a fight with each other and both are injured.

The officer in charge should arrange for medical treatment of the trustees. A full report of the incident should be made to the officer's superior for advice as to whether or not each of the trustees should be rearrested for mutual battery. If it is decided that arrests are in order, it is necessary to make the usual report. If it is decided that further arrests and bookings are not to be made, a written report of all facts surrounding the incident should be made.

57. An officer has a subpoena for a person, but the person refuses to identify himself to the officer. However, the officer believes he has the right person.

There is no legal requirement that a person submit identification to an officer. This makes the procedure of making service upon the right person a difficult thing in some situations. However, the officer can inquire of the neighbors, or persons who are acquainted with the subject, regarding the legal identification, such as weight, height, color of eyes and hair, etc. If the officer is certain that he has the right person, he should serve the subpoena in the manner prescribed by law.

59. A woman complains that her next door neighbor continually throws her refuse into the complainant's yard over a six foot fence.

The person should be advised of her rights to make a private person's arrest for the misdemeanor committed in her presence. If the person decides to make a physical arrest, the officer should abide by her desires. The officer could also take a crime report for dumping on private property under the appropriate city or county ordinance, and make application for complaint for a warrant of arrest. It is suggested that the officer talk to the neighbor and suggest that differences be ironed out in a more amicable fashion. In this connection, it could also be suggested that the neighbor retrieve the offending refuse, and that she desist from like actions.

60. An officer observes an elderly man with a white cane lying on the sidewalk. Nearby there is a "seeing eye" dog, unmuzzled. At the approach of the officer, the dog apparently confused and frightened, snarls in a vicious manner.

If it is apparent that the man is in need of medical attention an ambulance should be summoned immediately. The "seeing eye" dog has a harness on him which the officer could seize to keep the dog from biting anybody. Generally if the dog is allowed to accompany his master in the ambulance no further difficulty will occur. However, if it is apparent that the dog is not going to cooperate, the officer should isolate the dog and call for assistance from the pound or humane society in that area.

61. A man is found lying on a sidewalk with the side of his head crushed. From all appearances, and from statements made by witnesses, the man jumped or fell from about the 5th floor of a hotel.

In addition to following the procedure, as in situation 48, the officer should proceed as quickly as possible into the hotel and locate the room from which the person came. The officer could take the room clerk or manager with him to enter the room, but the clerk or manager should not be permitted to touch anything. The examination of the room should include considerations of:

1. A possible suicide
2. A possible homicide
3. A possible accidental fall

All three possibilities demand that all evidence be preserved, including any notes, evidence of more than one person occupying or being in the room, etc. Although it is not conclusive by any means, it has been found that a "leaper" suicide will jump away from a building, while a homicide or accidental fall will result in a body being found relatively close to the building.

Any personal effects left by the deceased should be booked or turned over to the coroner, after a receipt is obtained. If any money is found it should be counted in the presence of the room-clerk, the hotel manager, or any other reliable person, such as a newspaper reporter.

62. A person telephones to complain that a swarm of bees has taken over his back porch, making it impossible to exit or enter.

There may be other city or county agencies better prepared to handle this situation but public safety is a police function. Every effort should be made to remedy this hazardous condition, but no officer should tackle a swarm of bees unless he knows how to handle them. This is a good illustration of the need for being prepared before the situation arises, such as maintaining a list of policemen or private persons who are experienced in such matters. Many persons keep bees or collect honey for profit or as a hobby. The names and address of such persons should be kept on file at the station, along with those experienced in handling skunks, snakes, and so-forth. Such lists of persons have proved to be of invaluable assistance in emergencies.

63. Executing a raid.

1. The final phase of a raid consists of the approach, the check at the rendezvous, and the operation. The participants approach the rendezvous point as silently as possible. If the rendezvous point is close to the area to be raided, vehicles may be left some distance away under guard. If the raid is to be performed during the night, the personnel engaged in the raid should be examined for articles which may glow in the dark. A signal is given by each raider as he occupies his assigned position. Where necessary, roadblocks are established to obstruct or control movements of vehicles or pedestrians in the area to be raided. A cordon may be posted to prevent personnel, suspects, or witnesses from escaping, or to prevent nonpartici-pants from entering the area.

2. Communication between members of the raiding party may be made by voice or signal. Communications between the raiding party and suspects may be by telephone or public-address system. When a suspect or suspects, upon instruction on how to surrender, comply and leave the building or area, they should not be allowed to re-enter. They should be restrained immediate-

ly and subjected to a thorough search. Should the suspect, upon instruction, refuse to surrender, the building or premises will be entered. Those designated to enter will take advantage of all cover afforded by walls, hedges, and buildings until they reach the door of the building housing the suspect. When entering, they open the door with a hard push to insure there is no one hiding behind it, always remaining under the protection of the wall beside the door.

3. When the raid commander signals the completion of the raid, all members of the raiding party assemble at the designated place and are accounted for before the party leaves the scene of the raid. The raid commander may, when necessary, leave guards at the scene of the raid to observe or to apprehend accomplices of the suspects.

64. Preceding an election day an officer observes some political posters on telephone poles.

Many cities and counties have ordinances making it a misdemeanor to post advertising of any character, including political advertising, upon utility poles or public property. If such postings are witnessed by an officer the person should be arrested and all posters in his possession should be booked as evidence. The posted one should be removed by the officer and booked as evidence.

When the posting is not observed, but when the posters are observed posted on utility poles or public property, officers should remove such posters except when posted in such a manner, or the amount of postings are such, as to make their removal impractical. In the latter case, the officer should make a written report to indicate the location of the posters and the reason for nonremoval.

Departmental policy will indicate when to seek a complaint against the person, persons, or political party responsible for such illegal postings.

65. In responding to a "man down" call, an officer sees a crowd near an apparently dead body. It is determined that the body has been exposed to public view for about ten minutes.

When a dead body has been exposed to public view it should be covered, pending the arrival of the ambulance or coroner. In some instances the investigation of the crime (or suspected crime) scene will demand that the body remain in place until the necessary phases of the preliminary investigation have been completed, such as: identifying the body, locating witnesses, preserving the scene, taking custody of personal effects, assisting the coroner and detectives or follow-up investigators.

Public opinion must be considered in regard to how long the body should remain in public view. General experience reveals that a body should not remain in public view longer than thirty minutes. Only extraordinary circumstances would justify a longer period.

66. An officer witnesses a misdemeanor committed but the offender escapes. The next day the officer sees the offender and takes him into custody.

The general rule applying in misdemeanor arrest cases is that the arrest must be made at the time the offense or any part of the offense is being committed or within a reasonable time thereafter or upon fresh and immediate pursuit of the offender. Although no hard and fast rule can be laid down which will fit every case respecting what constitutes a reasonable time, it is safe to say that the officer must act promptly in making the arrest and as soon as possible under the circumstances.

Since no continued pursuit, nor other excuse for the delay exists, it would seem that the delay of a day erased the authority to arrest. It would be quite proper, however, to secure adequate identification, place of work and residence address, so that the officer could secure a warrant for the arrest. If the officer does not act immediately after the offense has been committed, he can thereafter make arrests only by procuring a warrant and proceeding in accordance with its terms.

67. Officers are informed that a Communist meeting is to take place at a certain location in their district.

Very few states have any laws regulating Communists or Communist meetings, but there are laws prohibiting the teaching, preaching, speaking or advocating the overthrow of the government by the use of force or violence. If the latter situation is suspected, an immediate report should be made by the officers to their superior officer, and, if possible, to the local office of the Federal Bureau of Investigation. Further and more complete investigations should be made by undercover or plainclothes investigators. The uniformed officers should not attempt to investigate or stop such meetings unless a specific, valid law prohibits such meetings.

68. An officer observes a low flying airplane "buzzing" a particular residential area.

The United States Civil Air Regulations cover many dangerous flying activities such as:
Section 60.16 prohibits acrobatic flight
  1. Over congested cities, towns, open air assembly of persons
  2. In a civil airway or control zone
  3. When flight visibility is less than three miles
  4. Below 1500 feet (from surface)
Section 60.12 prohibits *careless* or *reckless* operation
  1. Violation of this section usually involves violation of 60.16 above
Section 60.17 except in landing and taking off—NO AIRCRAFT SHALL FLY LOWER THAN:

1. One thousand feet over congested areas or open air assemblies (surface to aircraft)
2. Five hundred feet over open areas or sparsely settled areas (surface to aircraft)

Most departments specify that enforcement is the duty of the patrolman. The reporting, arrest and complaint procedures should be established by individual departments.

Altitude can be estimated: If the identification numbers can be read, the aircraft is *probably* below 700 feet. If facial details of the pilot can be defined (glasses, cap, helmet), the aircraft is probably below 500 feet. This latter estimation can be improved by noting or observing a pedestrian or a driver in a car at known distances.

69. The police officer investigating a routine traffic accident finds a gun in the glove compartment of the car involved.

This could amount to carrying a concealed weapon, a misdemeanor under a dangerous weapons control law, providing that the officer can prove a certain person was in possession of the car and its contents. If proof of possession is possible, the officer should make an arrest under the above law and book the gun as evidence. If no proof of possession is possible at the time, the gun should be seized, booked as evidence, and a full report made for follow-up investigation by the detectives as to the possibility of a gun of similar description being used in some major crime of record.

70. An officer receives a request for help from a woman whose cat is atop a fifty-foot tree.

The cat will usually come down when it gets hungry. If the cat remains in the tree for a considerable period of time, the officer should request assistance from the nearest animal shelter, humane society, pound, or the fire department.

71. Officers stop a pedestrian at 1:00 A.M. in a residential district for questioning. He refuses to give any identification. He is well dressed and states that he will sue the officers if they detain him or search him.

The right to stop, question, and search a person depends upon whether or not the public safety so demands. Many factors enter into "public safety," such as

1. Have crimes been committed in the area recently?
2. Does the pedestrian answer the description of any wanted person or suspect in a crime report?
3. Does the pedestrian give conflicting stories, or an evasive answer as to why he just "happens to be in the neighborhood?"
4. Did he act in a suspicious manner such as attempt to hide behind a

tree or telephone pole, throw something away on the approach of officers, etc.?

5. Did he attempt to flee or run from the officers?

72. Officers in responding to "a shooting" call find a victim seriously wounded. The victim tells the officers that "John Doe" had shot him, and then dies.

In criminal actions, the act or declaration of a dying person, made under a sense of impending death, respecting the cause of his death, is admissible. The primary test or characteristic of a dying declaration is the "sense of impending death," that is, the declarant must have abandoned all hope or expectation of living. If he had any hope of recovery at the time he made the statement, it is not admissible in evidence—such as, "believing that I am very near death, and that I may not recover."

Although belief of impending death may be inferred from such circumstances as his physical condition, the nature of his wounds or injuries, his knowledge of his condition, and his conduct, the officer should make appropriate notes as to the statements made as to his state of mind. These declarations or signs made by the dying person must relate to the cause of his injuries and to those matters having such a causal connection with the assault as to be a part of the occurrence.

73. An officer observes that a manhole cover is missing.

Requests for emergency service should be made when: (1) the cover is missing from a sewer manhole, (2) gas is escaping from a manhole or a drain inlet, or (3) an explosion occurs in a sewer manhole or a storm drain. Requests for the emergency services shall be made by telephone to the fire department (when a fire or fire hazard exists), and to the Department of Public Works, or by radio to the dispatcher, who will request assistance. Take safety precautions until the condition is remedied.

74. A citizen complains that he has just been the victim of false advertising.

Most states have laws regarding false advertising, which generally read as follows:

"Making or disseminating untrue or misleading statements is unlawful. It is unlawful for any person, firm, corporation or association, or any employee thereof with intent directly or indirectly to dispose of real or personal property or to perform services, professional or otherwise, or anything of any nature whatsoever or to induce the public to enter into any obligation relating thereto, to make or disseminate or cause to be made or disseminated before the public in this state, in any newspaper or other publication, or any advertising device, or by public outcry or proclamation, or in any other manner or means whatever, any statement, concerning such real or personal property or services, professional or otherwise, or concerning any circumstance or matter of fact connected with the proposed performance or disposition thereof, *which is untrue or misleading,* and which is known, or which by the exercise of reasonable care should be known, to be untrue or misleading."

"*Exception:* 17502. Application of article to broadcasting station or publisher acting in good faith. This article does not apply to any visual or sound radio broadcasting station or to any publisher of a newspaper, magazine, or other publication, who broadcasts or publishes an advertisement in good faith, without knowledge of its false, deceptive, or misleading character."

An interesting application of the above was decided in People vs. Wahl (1940)—39 Cal. App. 2nd Supp. 771 where a person advertised "Special sale of (named) tubes, 50 percent off regular firstline tube list price." As a matter of fact, the tubes were third line. In holding that this type of advertising was deceptive and misleading, the court held that there was a violation, even without any specific intent to deceive.

If the investigation indicates that an arrest of the advertiser should be made, the officer should do so. If the case appears to be borderline, the victim should be referred to the prosecuting attorney.

75. An injured person requests the services of a clergyman.

When a person suffering from an injury or illness requests the services of a clergyman, the dispatcher should be notified immediately. He should be notified whether the clergyman is to be directed to the scene of the incident, or to a particular hospital. (If investigation reveals that a seriously ill or injured person is of a particular religious denomination, but because of physical condition is unable to request a clergyman, the dispatcher should be notified as though a request had been made.) Clergymen and doctors should be permitted to approach dead or dying persons, but they should be cautioned to avoid destroying any evidence.

76. A person receives a minor injury and requests that a report be made of the injury.

An injury report form should be made when:
1. A unit is assigned to answer an ambulance call and the patient receives treatment at the scene or is removed to a hospital.
2. An illness or injury involves, or might involve further police investigation.
3. An illness or injury might result in liability to the city.
4. A person has attempted suicide.
5. A person has an epileptic or other type of seizure.

An injury report is not necessary when other police reports, such as traffic, arrest, or crime reports are made setting forth the circumstances of the injury. In epilepsy cases, an injury report should be made regardless of the making of other reports, because a copy should be sent to the motor vehicle licensing department.

A good rule: "When in doubt, make a written report."

77. A broken power or transmission line is in the street.

A power or transmission line which is broken or creates a hazardous condition should be reported to the agency responsible for correcting the condition. If the agency responsible is unavailable, take safety measures until the condition is remedied. Do whatever is practical, such as blocking off the street, setting up barricades, or using flares.

78. An officer observes a dangerous excavation on private property.

When a dangerous and unprotected excavation on private property is observed, the conditions should be reported by telephone to the building department. Take safety measures until the condition is remedied. Do what is practical, as indicated in problem 77.

79. An officer observes an abandoned icebox with a door on it.

An officer learning of a discarded or abandoned icebox, refrigerator, or deep freeze locker should:

1. Inform the owner, or person responsible for the hazard, and request him to take proper action to correct it.

2. When unable to locate the owner or person responsible, take appropriate action to correct any obvious hazard to children.

One state law provides:

"Any person who discards or abandons or leaves in any place accessible to children any refrigerator, icebox, or deep freeze locker, having a capacity of one and one-half cubic feet or more, which is no longer in use, and which has not had the door removed or the hinges and such portion of the latch mechanism removed to prevent latching or locking of the door is guilty of a misdemeanor. Any owner, lessee, or manager who knowingly permits such a refrigerator, icebox, or deep freeze to remain on premises under his control without having the door removed or the hinges and such portions of the latch mechanism removed to prevent latching or locking of the door, is guilty of a misdemeanor. Guilt of a violation of this section shall not, in itself, render one guilty of manslaughter, battery, or other crime against a person who may suffer death or injury from entrapment in such refrigerator, icebox, or deep freeze locker.

"The provisions of this section shall not apply to any vendor or seller of refrigerators, iceboxes, or deep freeze lockers, who keeps or stores them for sale purposes, if the vendor or seller takes reasonable precautions to effectively secure the door of any such refrigerator, icebox, or deep freeze locker, so as to prevent entrance by children small enough to fit therein."

80. Officers receive a major disaster broadcast.

Officer detecting disasters or emergencies which will involve a large segment of the population or cause them major inconvenience should:

1. Make a reconnaissance of the area.

2. Determine the nature of the disaster or emergency, its extent, and possible duration.

3. Telephone or transmit to the dispatcher all pertinent information, and request all necessary assistance.

81. An officer arrives at a scene where many people are injured.

Requests for immediate medical assistance at the scene of a major disaster or emergency should be made by either telephoning the emergency hospital or notifying the dispatcher by radio, and having him request necessary assistance. The dispatcher should maintain a file of hospitals, medical personnel, and ambulance services which may be called upon to supplement emergency hospital facilities.

Also, the officer(s) at the scene should:

1. Request additional police personnel as the situation may demand.

2. Request barricades, ropes, and lanterns as needed.

3. Protect the scene as much as possible until help arrives. Consider the possibility of using civilian volunteers.

82. A speaker has a permit to speak in a public park, but his speaking causes many people to block traffic in the street.

Under most state laws, anyone who participates in a crime is a principal, accomplice, or accessory to that crime. In this case, the direct act of the speaker is causing the blocking of traffic, thus making him a party to the blocking of traffic. However, the strict enforcement of the law in this instance must be done so there is complete recognition of the right to freedom of speech. While the person's freedom of speech should not be abridged or denied, still it must remain within the bounds of propriety. Thus, it would seem that the proper action would be to warn the speaker to move to a better location, and to warn those blocking the street that they may be subject to arrest. If either or both refuse to budge, then it would seem that arrests would be in order.

83. An officer is called to a post office where an employee states that a certain package is "ticking" and may contain explosives.

If the preliminary investigation reveals that dangerous materials (explosives, incendiary or caustic chemicals, etc.) are involved and a danger exists, every effort should be made to safeguard all persons from danger. Next, the services of a specialist in explosives should be obtained, and, pending his arrival, officers should be guided by his telephonic advice. Dangerous materials should not be transported or taken to any police premises, except when so directed by the specialist. If such a package is found aboard an airplane, it should not be permitted to take off, but instead, the area surrounding it should be isolated until the specialist is satisfied that the situation is SAFE!

84. An officer observes an air pollution violation.

When an officer observes a violation of an Air Pollution Control District regulation, he should notify the violator that such action is in violation of the particular regulation. If the violator fails to comply, such noncompliance shall be reported by the officer in a written report. The report shall include the:

1. Location
2. Time
3. Type or nature of the violation
4. Name of the violator.

The report shall be immediately forwarded to the enforcement officer of the APCD for enforcement and prosecution. In those jurisdictions where the police are charged with the enforcement of air pollution regulations, departmental procedures shall pertain.

85. An officer receives a call of someone shooting in the hills, within the city, and discovers a male juvenile with a 22 caliber rifle taking pot shots at tin cans in a gully.

There are usually no state laws covering this situation, but there is usually a city or county ordinance preventing the discharge of a firearm within the jurisdiction concerned. If so, the officer could make an arrest for the discharge of a firearm in his presence, or issue a warning or confiscate the gun and make application for filing the petition in the juvenile court. Discretion usually dictates the appropriate action to be taken.

86. A citizen complains that a junk dealer just beat his horse. The junk dealer tells the officers to mind their own business.

The citizen may be informed of his rights to make a private person's arrest. If the person does not wish to make an arrest, the officer should obtain a crime report from him and proceed by making application for complaint. If the marks on the horse are visible, the officer should obtain a photographer to take photos of the injuries to the animal and the junk dealer should not be allowed to take his horse from the scene until the photographs have been taken. If the injuries are severe, the officer should take action to insure treatment of the animal by a veterinarian.

87. A person complains that a restaurant has just served her some poisoned food.

In this situation, the officer should:
1. Call an ambulance, if an actual emergency exists.
2. If no emergency exists, advise her to see her own doctor.
3. Make a written report covering the facts of the situation, and have the complaining person sign the report.
4. Notify the Health Department without delay regarding all the facts of the case. The Health Department usually has a food sanitation specialist on duty who will pursue the matter according to the food laws of the state.
5. Preserve the remaining portion of the food for laboratory analysis.

88. The officer finds a person pinned under the wheels of a train, at the scene of an accident.

Besides calling an ambulance, the officer should secure the services of heavy equipment from the fire department, a crane company, a street car line, or the armed services. Usually this request for equipment is relayed by radio or telephone to communications, where telephone calls can be made to secure the assistance from the agency which can respond the quickest. The department should have information on agencies which have this type of equipment, and it should be always *available* to the dispatcher.

89. A citizen complains that a man is spitting on the sidewalk.

If the officer observes the violation, an arrest can be made. Otherwise, the private person may make an arrest, because such action constitutes "offensive conduct." This is usually defined in city or county ordinances as a misdemeanor. It is assumed in this situation that the spitting is intentional, and not any involuntary action by a person taken suddenly ill.

90. An officer answers an "assault with a deadly weapon" call aboard a ship in the harbor, and is ordered off the ship by the captain.

The general rule is that vessels within the territorial waters of the United States become subject to the laws thereof, in which case the captain would have no right to order the officer off the ship. When dealing with foreign vessels it would be appropriate to secure the assistance of the harbormaster in attempting to conduct a proper investigation. If the harbormaster is unavailable, then the Coast Guard may be called on for assistance.

91. An officer is informed that a person has aimed a gun at another person, stating, "I am going to kill you." The officer examines the gun, and finds no cartridges in the chamber, and verifies that the gun was empty at the time that the threat was made.

Attempting to shoot a person with an unloaded gun is not generally an assault with a deadly weapon or instrument (a felony) but it would constitute a misdemeanor in most states for "pointing a loaded or unloaded gun at another person in a threatening manner." Such actions may constitute a breach of the peace. The victim may make a private person's arrest or a crime report could be made and signed by the victim and a warrant of arrest obtained.

92. A woman threatens to commit suicide. A friendly neighbor goes to the drug store, buys some poison and gives it to the woman, who consumes it and dies as a result.

Although suicide isn't an illegal act in most states, the act of the "friendly" neighbor usually constitutes a felony. If sufficient evidence is available, the officer should proceed to arrest the neighbor for assisting in a suicide, or for a homicide. All evidence should be preserved and booked.

93. A man is found loitering near a schoolyard with lewd literature on his person.

The person is usually classified as a vagrant under most state laws, which read:

"Every person who loiters about any school or any place at or near which school children attend is vagrant and is punishable by a fine of not exceeding five hundred dollars ($500) or by imprisonment in the county jail for not exceeding six months, or by both such fine and imprisonment."

In this situation, the person should be placed under arrest and booked. The names of teachers or children who observed the loitering should be obtained and incorporated in the arrest report. It is sometimes possible to secure a crime report from whomever observed the loitering.

94. A church member of a "minority" group calls an officer to his home at midnight and shows him a burning cross planted in the center of his lawn. Two nineteen year old boys of the same "minority" group later confess they committed the act as a joke.

Such an act is inimical to the public welfare, and should not be condoned or tolerated. A crime report should be taken from the church member, and a complaint should be obtained and a warrant issued for the arrest of the wrongdoers. The remains of the burned cross should be booked as evidence. Sometimes photographs should also be taken as evidence.

95. An officer observes a citizen holding a person he states has just thrown a brick through a department store window.

Such action is malicious mischief, for which the person could be arrested by the person who saw the act committed, and in his presence. This would be a private person's arrest, and the procedure followed should be according to departmental regulations. If there are indications that a burglary was intended, the arrest should be made for an intended felony.

96. A person complains to an officer that his neighbors are planning to cut

his water hose because water ran onto their properties, and that they have purchased a hatchet to be used in the deed.

Except in conspiracy cases, the mere preparation to commit a crime is not a crime. An attempt to commit a crime consists of two elements:
1. A specific intent to commit a particular crime, and
2. A direct act done toward its completion.

Under the facts of this case, it would seem that no crime has been committed, hence an arrest would not be in order. It is suggested that the officer talk to the neighbors and relate the complaint and suggest that they settle their differences in an amicable and legal manner. The officer should make a complete and written report of the incident for departmental records.

97. A woman reports to an officer that her neighbor intentionally sprayed her with his garden hose.

Such an act constitutes a battery. The victim should be informed of her rights to make a private person's arrest for the battery committed upon her, and if she makes an arrest, the departmental regulations relative to such an arrest should be followed. It is always possible, of course, to take a crime report for a battery from the victim for the officer to use in making an application for complaint against the suspect.

98. The president of a corporation files a theft report that an officer of the corporation is suspected of stealing materials from the corporation.

This type of situation is best handled by detectives. The detectives will usually follow the procedure of using tracing powder or dyes, plus some form of stakeout. If you are assigned to handle the situation, it is best to check with someone who is familiar with using such powder so it can be applied to property which may be involved in the next theft.

99. A property owner intentionally sets fire to an old building on his land, and the building is covered by insurance.

Such an act is considered to be arson, a felony, under most state laws, which read in general:

"Any person who willfully and maliciously sets fire to or burns or causes to be burned or who aids, counsels, or procures the burning of any dwelling house, or any kitchen, shop, barn, stable or other outhouse that is a parcel thereof, or belonging to or adjoining thereto, *whether the property of himself or another,* shall be guilty of arson, and upon conviction thereof, be sentenced to the penitentiary for not less than two or more than twenty years."

If the essential elements of the above-mentioned law are present, the person should be arrested for arson. If there is any doubt as to the elements of the corpus delicti, a full written report should be made of the facts and presented to the prosecuting attorney for his decision as to whether or not to prosecute.

In some states a fire permit may be obtained to destroy an old structure.

100. At the scene of a fire, a fire chief tells an officer to "arrest that man, I've seen him at the last three fires."

Standing alone, this statement would be insufficient to justify an arrest by the officer. But the fire chief could be questioned as to what other facts he has which would cause him to conclude that this particular person set the fires. It would be quite appropriate, and necessary, to interview the suspect as to his reasons for being at the scene, and how he learned about the fire, where he lives in relation to the fire, etc. He should also be interviewed along the same lines regarding his presence at other fires. If no satisfactory answers are given, it would seem that reasonable or probable cause for making an arrest would exist, hence the person should be taken into custody. When there is doubt as to the person's connection with the fires, a complete report of the interviews should be made after the officer concludes his investigations. This report is usually sent to the unit handling arson investigations, which, in many cities, is in the fire department.

101. An officer receives a request for help from a woman who is locked out of her apartment.

Generally, it is possible to secure a duplicate key from the owner or manager of the apartment house. In lieu thereof, the officer could check in the phone book for an all-night locksmith for the woman if she so desires. Other methods of assistance could be rendered, such as slipping the lock with a plastic card, prying open a window or screen, or securing the services of an officer experienced in locks.

102. A pervert is cruelly beaten up by two men, who accompanied him to his room.

This is commonly known as a "fruit roll," and may be a felony, depending on the severity of the injuries sustained. In any event, a crime report should be taken and investigation made. Sometimes the suspects may be in the vicinity of wherever they met the pervert, in which case it would be proper to take the victim to that general vicinity for a possibility of an on-the-spot arrest. The case should be referred to the vice officer for a follow-up investigation, if the investigation is not completed by the officer.

103. A citizen complains to police that he has received many threatening telephone calls during the past week.

Threatening telephone calls constitute at least a disturbance of the peace, a misdemeanor, and a crime report should be taken of the incidents. It is possible to trace such calls, although the procedure requires the cooperation of the telephone company and considerable expense to have that particular line monitored. This latter action can only be authorized by the telephone company, over which the police have no control. It may be possible to tape record the conversation by means of an induction coil placed under the telephone, which is now considered legal. The induction coil leads to a loud speaker attachment.

If the victim recognizes the voice of the culprit, then an application could be made and a warrant could be obtained for the arrest of said person.

104. While waiting to testify in a misdemeanor case an officer suddenly remembers one essential element he did not personally observe and which, in all probability, would be necessary to obtain a conviction.

The Prosecuting Attorney should be immediately informed of this fact. It may be that there is a witness to establish the missing part of the corpus delicti. If a witness is not present the Prosecuting Attorney could ask for a continuance of the case in order to locate a witness. In any event, all of the facts should be presented to the judge or jury for consideration and decision. Under no circumstances should a person try to bluff his way through a prosecution because the duty of an officer is dual in character: to protect the innocent and prosecute the guilty.

105. The number of robberies and burglaries in a particular locality are so great that the police agency has decided to conduct an unlimited number of "police blockades."

Under this situation a "police blockade" is defined as blocking off designated areas and stopping all persons and automobiles entering or leaving such areas and searching them without first obtaining a search warrant. The general rule is that persons lawfully within the United States are entitled to use the public highways and have a right to free passage thereon without interruption or search, unless a public officer authorized to search, knows of probable cause for believing that the vehicle is carrying contraband or that the occupants thereof have violated some law. Unless probable cause exists in a particular situation (such as a recent robbery or kidnapping, followed by an immediate search and "blocking off" of the concerned area) it would seem that any wholesale and indiscriminate "police blockade" would be contrary to the provisions of the 4th Amendment of the Constitution of the United States.

DISTURBANCES OF THE PEACE

106. Officers answer a "disturbing the peace" call, and upon arrival the wife wants her husband arrested for drunkenness.

Under most city or county ordinances it is a crime to be drunk on private property to the annoyance of another person. Under such an ordinance a wife can make a so-called "citizen's" arrest or "private person's" arrest of her husband. However, if the disturbance is committed in the presence of the officers, they may arrest and record the wife or others as complaining witnesses who were annoyed. In this latter situation it would be advisable to obtain a signed crime report from the wife.

107. Officers answer a "woman screaming" call, and upon arrival, find that a husband has struck his wife in the face.

This type of action is usually a felony under the state laws constituting "wife beating." The wording of these sections is usually broad enough to cover any bodily harm caused by the application of force. A crime report should be taken from the wife before the husband is booked for wife beating. If the wife is reluctant to sign the crime report, an arrest can nevertheless be made, since a crime is an offense against the people rather than against an individual. Some departments suggest that the wife be taken to an emergency hospital for medical treatment and then to the photography laboratory for photographs of the injured area. However, this must be done voluntarily on the part of the wife, as she may legally refuse both medical treatment and having her photograph taken. If the wife does not appear to be seriously injured and she states that she does not wish to prosecute or have her husband arrested, the officers may warn the husband, write a summary of the action taken, and leave. Caution should be exercised during this latter police action because a wife will sometimes make such a statement in the presence of her husband because of fear of what he might do. It would be appropriate to take the wife to one side and question her out of the hearing of her husband.

It is never a condition precedent to an arrest that a crime report be obtained, since crimes are offenses against the people of a state, and not a matter of discretion on the part of a victim as to whether or not he wishes to prosecute.

108. Officers receive a disturbance call and upon arrival see a man discharging firecrackers. The person states that he is Chinese and it is their custom to shoot off firecrackers in celebration of the opening of a new store, but admits that he does not have a permit to discharge fireworks.

This is a technical violation, but a violation nevertheless. Discretion will indicate whether to make an arrest. Suggest the delaying of the celebration until a permit is obtained or instruct him to conclude his celebration as soon as possible and make a written report of the incident. If an arrest is made, the firecrackers should be seized as contraband and booked as evidence.

109. Officers are assigned to maintain order in a public park during a Fourth of July celebration at which about 5,000 persons are in attendance.

A group of seven or eight persons are drinking beer in the park in violation of a local ordinance.

In group celebrations the possibility for violations to occur increases in direct proportion to the numbers present. It is suggested that the first step the officers should take should be to explain to the group the law prohibiting drinking and request that they drink elsewhere. It is not recommended that the beer be seized unless an arrest is made. It would seem that since this is a happy occasion there should be no thought of arresting anyone except as a last possible method of obtaining compliance with the ordinance.

110. An officer answers a "loud party" call and finds present an obnoxious drunk who turns out to be a neighbor of one of the officers.

Generally speaking the presence of an officer at the scene of a loud party is merely adventitious. The courts take a dim view of officers attempting to enforce a disturbance of the peace law in a party situation. The fact that there is a drunk present who is a neighbor of one of the officers should not influence him in making a correct disposition. This means that the legal procedures should be followed and the officer should inform the other persons present that if they wish to arrest the drunk person (assuming there is a city or county ordinance covering this situation) they should do so. If the crime is committed in the presence of the officer then he could make a physical arrest. As far as drunks are concerned the general attitude is that a person should not be arrested for drunk unless he is so far under the influence of intoxicating liquor as to be unable to care for himself. If there are other persons present who can take care of him there is no good reason why he could not be released to their custody. This is just another way of saying that officers are paid to protect lives and property regardless of who is involved.

111. In response to a call regarding a family disturbance an officer finds the male participant to be a "great friend of police officers." The wife accuses him of striking her and demands arrest be made immediately as she points to a black eye. Both parties "had been drinking."

Family arguments are probably the cause of the most headaches to police officers. Generally the wife has a legitimate complaint against the husband but she is usually a reluctant witness the next morning. Police officers should attempt to reconcile the parties if possible. Failing this, the officers could advise the wife of her rights to arrest her husband for a crime committed against her. The fact that the husband is a "great friend of the police" does not entitle him to any special privilege and any preferential treatment would be unprofessional conduct on the part of any officer.

112. An officer answers a "disturbing the peace" call, and is met by a woman who has a small cut on her forehead, but the bathroom in her

home has a considerable amount of blood in it. The woman refuses medical attention, does not want to make a report, and will only tell the officer that a man broke into her apartment.

If the woman remains adamant, the officer should leave the premises, but make a written report regarding the circumstances. Some attempt should be made by the officer to locate the person who made the original call to the department. It may be that the complainant has additional information upon which the officer could act.

If a person's life is not in danger, that person may legally refuse to receive medical attention and there is no legal requirement compelling a person to make a criminal or any other type of report to the police department in this type of situation.

113. The city has an anti-noise ordinance. The members of a wedding party are blowing auto horns early in the afternoon, to the annoyance of the person who complained to the officer.

The general procedure would be to do nothing unless there is a complainant. Even with a complainant, the officer would be exercising good judgment if he proceeded to warn the wedding party about a violation of the ordinance before taking any action. It would seem that only an extreme abuse in blowing auto horns would justify any more action than a warning, due to the inherent nature of the situation.

114. A radio car officer receives a call to go to the ball park and see the manager. Upon arrival, he observes a major disturbance of the peace in the ball park with hundreds of people involved in fights and seat cushions and bottles being thrown.

There are certain procedures to be followed when there is a major disturbance of the peace:
  1. Call for assistance before taking action.
  2. Use the public address system to announce:
     a. "This is the police."
     b. "This is a misdemeanor."
     c. "Cease and desist immediately."
  3. Repeat, three or four times.
  4. Have a plainclothes officer go to the far end of the stadium and signal if you can be heard.
  5. If the above is ineffective, make arrests of as many as possible.
  6. Such actions may also constitute unlawful assembly or a riot.

115. An officer answers a "shots fired" call, and upon arrival the occupants of the house deny that shots were fired. The nearby neighbors state that they heard a shotgun, but upon rechecking, the occupants still deny hearing any shots.

The officer should first question the complainant regarding the possibility of the noise being a sonic boom, auto backfire, or a loud TV or radio. The officer should also question other persons in the neighborhood as to whether they heard possible shots fired. In this manner, the officer may be able to ascertain whether this is a "crank call" or is a bona fide complaint. If the persons interviewed are apparently sincere and evidence reliability, then the officer could be justified in conducting a search of the premises for a possible felony. If the officer decides that there is not sufficient evidence to support a search being made, he should at least make a written report of the incident and the accompanying circumstances.

116. An officer answers a disturbance of the peace call where neighbors complain that a religious meeting is very disturbing.

Noisy religious meetings may be disturbing, but since their intention is not to violate any laws, it is doubtful whether any arrest should be made. Instead, the officer should contact the original complainant and others in the neighborhood and then proceed to contact the person in charge of the meeting. The person in charge should be informed regarding the complaint and a request for moderation should be made. If this complaint continues, the complainant should be referred to the office of the prosecuting attorney, who could hold an office hearing before any criminal proceedings are instituted.

117. An officer is called to an office building or business establishment. The person in charge states that the building has been closed for one hour and an irate citizen refuses to leave.

The officer should question the citizen as to why he refuses to leave, being alert as to the possibility that the person is either drunk, covering up for a burglary, or is merely disturbing the peace. Inquiry should disclose what violations may be involved and in any event the person in charge may charge the person with a violation of disturbing the peace and make an arrest accordingly.

118. An officer answers a call to "see the woman and keep the peace." The woman invites the officer into the house, but the husband refuses the officer admittance, and will not permit his wife to leave.

If tact and diplomacy fail, the officer should advise both parties concerned that a wilful detention of another person may constitute false imprisonment, which under some state laws reads as follows:

"False imprisonment is punishable by a fine not exceeding five hundred dollars or by imprisonment in the county jail not more than one year, or by both. If such false imprisonment be effected by violence, menace, fraud, or deceit, it shall be punishable by imprisonment in the state prison for not less than one nor more than ten years."

Of course, the officer should attempt to ascertain the reason why the call was made and handle it accordingly before taking action on the false imprisonment charge. Part of the corpus delicti of false imprisonment would be holding the wife against her will, which would necessitate obtaining a crime report from her to the effect that she was being held against her will before an arrest of the husband could be made.

119. At 3:00 a.m., several people in a neighborhood complain about heavy equipment working on a nearby construction project.

A practical solution would be for the officers to attempt to effect a mutual understanding between the construction company and the neighbors, such as by inquiring of the construction company as to how long the noise will continue, and then ask if the neighbors could forego the temporary inconvenience for that period of time, since by doing so they will be contributing to the expeditious completion of the project.

If arbitration fails, the officers could quote the existence of some city or county ordinance, such as the Los Angeles Municipal Code, a section which prohibits the using of power tools or machines between the hours of 9:00 p.m. to 7:00 a.m. to the annoyance of persons. However, exceptions are written into such ordinances to provide for construction and repairs during such prohibited hours with written permission of the Board of Police Commissioners, or Department of Public Works.

Generally, physical arrests are not deemed advisable, but it would certainly be proper to ask the parties concerned to appear in the office of the prosecuting attorney for an office hearing if other means failed to satisfactorily solve the problem.

120. An apartment manager complains that a tenant is drunk and disorderly in his own apartment. The manager doesn't want to make a personal arrest, and the tenant stopped making noise upon the arrival of the police.

An officer cannot arrest for a misdemeanor unless he has reasonable cause to believe that the person to be arrested has committed a misdemeanor in his presence. In this situation, the manager should be advised regarding these limitations upon an officer in making a misdemeanor arrest. Since there are no facts present which would give an officer a right to make a misdemeanor arrest, the manager should be advised regarding his rights to make an arrest for a misdemeanor committed in his presence. The officer should be guided by the wishes of the manager as to whether or not the manager wishes to make an arrest. If the manager does not wish to make an arrest, the officer should note the facts in his daily log or notebook and resume patrol. If the manager decides to make an arrest, the officer should tell the manager to place the person under arrest and after receiving the person into custody, the officer should then take a crime and an arrest report from the manager and book the arrestee to the manager. The manager should be informed that he may be required to testify in court, and must appear before the prosecuting attorney to sign a complaint.

121. A woman complains that her former boy friend insists on calling on her in an attempt to get her to go out with him.

The persistent annoying of a person constitutes "offensive conduct" under disturbance of the peace, a misdemeanor. Since this crime was not committed in the presence of the officer, the woman should be advised as to her right to make an arrest herself, if she so desires. In this event a stake-out could be arranged for apprehension of the suspect or a crime report could be taken and an application for the issuance of a warrant of arrest could be made by the woman.

122. An officer observes a man standing close to women window shoppers looking down at his feet. The man has an automobile rear view mirror tied to his shoe so he can look up the women's skirts.

The man is committing a disturbance of the peace. In this situation the officer may arrest the man. The officer should secure the names of witnesses, if any, and secure the name and address of the victims even though they may be unaware of the action, because they can at least testify as to the time and place.

123. In answering a disturbance of the peace call, an officer finds that it is a neighborhood argument, and both parties insist on a citizen's arrest of the other.

Both parties may arrest each other. In such an event, the officer should take a crime and an arrest report from each person and book each person to the other. Many times persons will demand the right to arrest each other at the scene and then when they get to the station, they change their minds and want to forget the whole thing. In the latter case, the officer should release the persons but make a written report regarding the incident.

124. In answering a "disturbance of the peace" call the owner of the premises points a gun at the officer and orders him to leave.

The owner of the property could order the officer to leave, but not at the point of a gun. Such action constitutes a misdemeanor under state laws, which generally read:

"Every person who, except in self defense, in the presence of any other person, draws or exhibits any firearm, whether loaded or unloaded, or any other deadly weapon whatsoever, in a rude, angry, or threatening manner, or who in any manner, unlawfully uses the same in any fight or quarrel, is guilty of a misdemeanor."

If there is a violation of the above mentioned section, the person should be disarmed, arrested, and booked. If the gun is loaded, there is a possibility that the person is guilty of an assault with a deadly weapon, a felony.

125. An aggressive salesman refuses to leave the front porch of a house where he is attempting to sell to the wife. The husband becomes irked and knocks the salesman off the porch with one punch.

In most states, it is held that refusing to leave the premises in such a situation is "offensive conduct," a disturbance of the peace, which is a misdemeanor. However, the mere commission of a misdemeanor does not usually justify the commission of another misdemeanor. The husband has committed a battery upon the salesman, which is also a misdemeanor. The parties may be advised as to their mutual rights to make mutual arrests of each other for these particular crimes. If each arrests the other, the officer should then take a crime report and an arrest report from each one before booking one to the other. The husband has a right to eject a person from his premises, but it must be done without excessive force.

126. A citizen complains that his neighbor is having a loud party, and he thinks that he has a slot machine in his garage.

The loud party may constitute a disturbance of the peace, for which the complainant may make an arrest of those persons who are causing the disturbance. The officer should not take part in the arrest for the loud party, because their presence there is merely a happenstance. The courts usually take a dim view of an officer making an arrest in such a situation, hence the prosecuting attorney in the area should be contacted for a ruling as to whether or not the officer should participate in such arrests. As to the slot machine, the mere possession of such a device is usually a misdemeanor except in states in which they are legal. The person in charge of the slot machine could be arrested for possessing it, and the machine could be booked as evidence.

127. Upon answering a disturbance of the peace call, an officer finds a relative has committed an assault and battery.

An assault is a misdemeanor. If the misdemeanor was not committed in the presence of the officer, he cannot make a legal arrest. If such is the case, the arrest must be made by the victim or a witness to the crime. If an arrest is made by either of the latter, the officer is obliged to receive the person in custody. A crime report should be taken from the victim.

128. In answering a disturbance of the peace, at a party, the officer finds that a nineteen-year-old couple is having a wedding party. He observes liquor on the table, but he does not observe anyone drinking. Some adults are present. The young husband orders the officer from the premises.

In this situation, it is advisable to locate the complainant, and advise him as to his rights to make a citizen's arrest. The officer should then proceed to the place where the party is in progress and advise the owner or person in charge that a complaint has been received. When the officer is ordered from the premises, he should leave unless an arrest is made. This is not to suggest that an arrest should be made, because the courts usually frown upon officers making an arrest at a party, especially a wedding party, where discretion dictates that a courteous and strategic withdrawal should be made.

HUSBAND AND WIFE PROBLEMS

129. A husband and wife agree to disagree and live separately. When he returns to get his clothes the wife won't let him in the house to get anything.

Generally, the husband has as much right to enter the premises as the wife has, unless there is a court order to the contrary. In this situation, the officer should warn both parties that the officer is there merely to preserve the peace and not to settle a civil dispute. If there is a fight or a disturbance committed in the presence of the officer, the one or ones who participate in this illegal activity should be arrested for disturbing the peace.

130. A husband and wife are separated but not divorced. They are living apart, but the husband returned during the absence of the wife and smashed the television set and the radio and stopped up the plumbing. The wife demands that the officers arrest him for something.

Since the items are probably community property, no crime has been committed. If any of the separate property of the wife has been destroyed, she could make a so-called "citizen's or private person's" arrest for the misdemeanor of malicious mischief, which in some state laws provides: "Every person who maliciously injures or destroys any real or personal property not his own, in cases otherwise than such as are specified in this code, is guilty of a misdemeanor." If the wife has a court order to the effect that the husband shall not bother her such actions would constitute a misdemeanor. If there was a court order, there would also be a contempt of court. Officers may arrest for violations of court orders, but should ascertain that a court order in fact exists and that there are no modifications thereof.

131. An officer on patrol is stopped by a woman who states she is leaving her husband, but he refuses to let her take the children and he intends to leave the state with them.

Under the facts stated, no crime has been committed. It is a civil problem for which the person should be referred to an attorney, or the civil division of the prosecuting attorney's office. If the children are of sufficient age to refuse being taken, it might possibly constitute kidnapping or child stealing, which are usually classified as felonies. If the latter situation prevails, the officer may proceed as in the handling of any other felony, but he should not take a police action unless a clear cut criminal case exists.

132. An officer answers a disturbing the peace call. A man has thrown his wife's clothing on the front lawn and refuses to let her into the house.

Generally, this is considered a civil matter, and the wife should be advised to see her attorney. No crime is involved unless someone is creating a disturbance. The officer should advise the wife to stay with some relative or girl friend, or if she has none, there are several agencies where she might stay overnight, such as a Salvation Army quarters, a Y.W.C.A., or some Community Chest agency.

A complete report should be made on the incident.

133. A husband complains that his wife has installed a "bug" or microphone in his house.

Most state laws and decisions now make the unauthorized installation of a recording machine a misdemeanor or prevent the introduction of any information gained thereby inadmissible under the Exclusionary Rule. This rule prevents any evidence from being produced in court which was secured in an illegal or unreasonable manner.

But there is no objection to the installation of a "bug" or recording machine in your own home or place of business. Some inquiry should be made as to whether any domestic difficulties exist—it may be that the other spouse may have put in the "mike" in order to gather evidence for divorce purposes. In such situations the persons should be left to settle their own affairs between themselves.

If an illegal installation is suspected then a "stakeout" or a "plant" might be instituted to apprehend the violator.

134. A woman complains that her common-law husband has returned to their home, although they have been separated several months, and removed their three-year-old daughter. She wishes him arrested for child stealing.

Many statutes pertaining to child stealing provide: "Every person who maliciously, forcibly or fraudulently takes or entices away any minor child *with intent to detain and conceal* such child from its parent, guardian, or other person having the lawful charge of such child, is punished by imprisonment in the state prison not exceeding twenty years."

Under such a statute the specific intent to detain and conceal must be proven. The facts of this case do not indicate this part of the corpus delicti, hence an arrest cannot be made under this law.

However, some consideration should be given to making an arrest under the general kidnapping laws. Some states do not provide for common-law marriages within their jurisdiction, hence the so-called "common-law husband" may not be a husband at all, therefore, it would seem that he would be classified as one not entitled to custody, and, hence, a kidnapper.

If the person is really her separated husband it would not be child stealing nor kidnapping unless a court order or law directed that the mother had legal custody to the exclusion of the husband.

135. A woman puts in a call for an officer, and upon his arrival, her husband orders them to leave the house.

Before leaving the premises, the officer should ascertain why he was called to the location, and be assured that there is no impending danger to the woman. If it is a mere domestic squabble, the officer should make a tactical withdrawal with discretion, leaving the unhappily wedded persons to their own devices.

136. An officer receives a disturbance of the peace call. Upon arrival at the address, the officer finds that the husband has locked his wife out of the house and will not allow her to re-enter. She is equally adamant that the officer force him to allow her in. She has no nearby relatives or friends.

The officer has no legal right to force the husband to allow the woman in. It is suggested that the officer try persuasion, and if this fails, some attempt should be made to locate a friend with whom the wife could stay for the remainder of the night. If both fail, then the Salvation Army or some other charitable organization may provide a place for her to stay. The officer should advise the wife to obtain legal advice from an attorney.

137. A newly-married woman complains to police that her husband is still married to another woman.

A bigamy report should be taken and turned over to the detectives for follow-up investigation. If the detectives are available, it might be advisable to have the woman interrogated by them. It may be that there would be sufficient information obtained so that an arrest for bigamy could be made. Since there must be proof of two marriages, the husband should be interrogated and asked what he did by way of dissolving the first marriage before consummating the second. In short, it would not seem advisable to arrest a person merely on the say-so of the second wife, without further investigation.

138. An irate husband reports that his wife has stolen the family car.

Generally speaking, a husband or wife can not be guilty of stealing if the property involved is classified as community property. Under some circumstances, or conditions, property ostensibly belonging to husband and wife could be the separate property of one or the other. In view of this, it would seem proper to take a miscellaneous crime report with a caption "Possible

Auto Theft," and present the facts to the prosecuting attorney for his opinion and possible issuance of a complaint. Unless there are unusual facts which would classify the car as separate property instead of community property, no complaint would be issued.

139. A woman complains that her divorced husband has left for a city in another state with an eighteen-year-old girl, and the final decree has not been granted.

The information should be recorded with the department, and a résumé of the facts could be sent by teletype to the other city police for a possible bigamy investigation. The FBI should also be contacted, and the facts related to them for a possible investigation for violation of the federal Mann act. This latter act relates to the transportation of a female across a state line for immoral purposes, a federal felony.

DRUNKENNESS

140. A wife complains that her husband is perpetually drunk and wants him committed for being an alcoholic.

The general procedure is to book the person for being drunk and advise the wife to appear in court at the time the husband is scheduled to appear. She can then inform the judge regarding the difficulty she is having and it may be possible for the court to order him to join Alcoholics Anonymous or some other organization as a condition of probation. It may be advisable to have the wife consult a mental counsellor regarding this situation. It is generally agreed that a person cannot become a reformed person unless he has the will to reform, thus the need for a commitment or assistance.

141. A male person who has been drinking considerably complains that "two guys just strong-armed me and took my money and then ran away."

Determine the victim's state of intoxication. If he is able to tell a coherent story and give a description, handle in the usual manner and take a robbery report. If the victim is unable to tell a coherent story, arrest him for drunk and include in the report that the victim claims that he had been robbed prior to arrest, but is unable to tell a coherent story.

142. On election day an officer observes a drunk person staggering up the front walk to a house displaying the American flag. The person states that he is going to vote at that location.

If sufficiently sober to vote, he should be allowed to vote, but if the person is too drunk to vote, he should be placed under arrest for drunkenness. The condition of the person will dictate what action the officer should take under the circumstances. American custom and law both provide for the opportunity and exercise of voting rights. The officer should in no way impede the exercise of the rights unless the individual is interfering with the orderly process of voting.

143. An officer answers a call at 3:00 a.m. to find a man drunk and down, unable to care for himself. The man is in a hallway by his upstairs apartment. Very young children can be heard crying inside. He refuses to tell where his keys are, no one answers the doorbell, and the manager of the building is not available.

The intoxicated person should be arrested and booked for violation of the law or ordinance violated. At the same time, adequate arrangements should be made for the proper care of the children. Entry to the room may be achieved by using lock picks or by securing the services of a locksmith.

If the mother or a reliable relative cannot be located, a juvenile detention place or a social service agency could be utilized to care for the children, pending the release of the father.

Departmental policy will dictate whether to file an additional charge for child neglect.

144. An officer observes an ice cream vendor on a three-wheeled bicycle wandering erratically in the street. Upon talking to the vendor, it becomes evident that he is drunk or had been drinking an alcoholic beverage.

Some state laws list such actions as "drunk driving," or "driving under the influence of intoxicating liquor." In any event, the person should be given a sobriety test, if he is able to take one. The names and addresses of witnesses may also be obtained. If it is determined that the person is in violation of a state or local ordinance he should be booked accordingly. In addition, the cycle should be impounded and the ice cream placed in cold storage until the subject is released. If the arrestee is an employee, it may be possible to contact the owner and release the cycle and its contents to the owner.

145. An individual is found in a drunken stupor in the front seat of his automobile. During the investigation the man's wife comes out of a nearby house and claims he consumed the alcohol in their house and that she sent him out to sleep in the car because of a domestic quarrel.

A practical solution would be to assist the wife in carrying the husband back into the house. If this is done then appropriate written reports should be made regarding the circumstances thereof. If departmental procedure has taken advantage of the new laws of arrest the person could be taken to the station for a "sobering up" period before being released. This law is now covered in California under Penal Code Section 849(b): "Any peace officer may release from custody, instead of taking such person before a magistrate, any person arrested without a warrant whenever: (2) 'The person arrested for intoxication only, and no further proceedings are desirable.'"

146. An officer is approached by two women who state they are members of "Alcoholics Anonymous." They ask the officer to assist them by taking another woman (who is in her own apartment, drunk) to the general hospital for commitment to a state institution for alcoholics. The two women state that the woman was released from the institution a week previously and placed in their custody. The woman begs the officer not to take her.

It is not the policy of "Alcoholics Anonymous" to arrest anyone. Their policy is to send rehabilitated drinkers to the person concerned for encouragement and assistance. It would seem that the two complainants were not bona fide members of the Alcoholics Anonymous.

147. While working alone, an officer attempts to bring a drunk to the station. The drunk is a bigger man and threatens that he won't go without a fight. When he is ordered to move, he pulls out a bottle and starts drinking again.

The recommended procedure would be to go to the call box or radio and request assistance before taking any further action. Upon the arrival of help, the officers could then proceed to forcibly subdue the belligerent drunk and arrest him for the appropriate drunk section and for resisting arrest.

If no help is forthcoming, the officer may forcibly take the drunk into custody and restrain him. If the drunk physically attacks the officer, then the officer may use any defensive means at his disposal to protect himself.

148. A person is found rolling around and kicking on a sidewalk, apparently drunk, but the officer detects no odor of alcohol on his breath. The officer suspects that the person is experiencing an epileptic seizure.

When a person either complains that he is a diabetic suffering from insulin shock, or appears to be in a coma, or appears to be in or recovering from a seizure, the officer should arrange to have the person taken immediately to a hospital. If the doctor confirms that the person is merely drunk or intoxicated, the person should be arrested and booked accordingly. But the person should be released from custody when the doctor states that the person is not intoxicated, but is merely suffering from (1) insulin shock, or the effects of some drug taken under the prescription and direction of a doctor, or (2) any illness or injury in which symptoms resemble those of intoxication.

149. An officer arrests an apparently intoxicated person who has no identification. During the booking procedure the drunk has "passed out," and the officer is unable to obtain information as to his name, address, age, or relatives.

Such a person is usually booked as "John Doe" until his true identification is established. But it would seem that the more immediate action to take would be to secure the services of a doctor to ascertain whether medical attention is necessary. The results of the doctor's examination should be noted on the arrest report, including what medical services were rendered.

150. A beat officer arrests a drunk and patrol wagon officers release him. The arresting officer calls you and it is discovered that the person isn't drunk. What action?

Under most state laws it is possible to arrest a person for more than one offense. Sometimes a person has not only been drinking but he has also been guilty of disturbing the peace. In such situations it is possible to arrest for either offense and thereafter prosecute for either or both offenses. This means that if an officer has arrested a person for drunk and delivered him to other officers for transportation to jail it would seem that the transporting officers should inquire as to the actual arrest situation before releasing him. Because, as explained, he may have another charge pending against him or there may be a difference of opinion as to sobriety. What is suggested here pertains to all situations that a proper investigation must first occur before any action is taken.

151. Officers in responding to a "fire" call in an apartment house discover that an elderly person, who had been drinking, fell asleep while smoking and set fire to the bed.

Being drunk in one's own residence is not usually considered an offense unless some other person is annoyed thereby. Even if such were the fact, this situation does not indicate that an arrest and booking would be desirable. Instead, preventive measures could be taken, such as the removal of all matches, and alerting the department manager or neighbors to be watchful of this person's apartment. Perhaps someone could be requested to furnish some coffee. Discretion will dictate what other steps could be taken.

Officers should make a note of this event in their notebook or daily log and resume patrol.

152. An officer answers a "drunk" call and finds a very drunken person who complains that his pocket was picked in a nearby bar. The interview discloses that the alleged victim is a clergyman.

Generally, drunks are unreliable witnesses and reports are not usually taken from them until they have sobered up sufficiently to relate their story in a coherent manner. The fact that the person is a clergyman should not create any special problem. The drunk should be handled as any other drunk. This means that if there is a sober person present who can take care of him and see him safely home, the drunk may be released to his care. If such a situation does not exist, the person should be arrested and booked. The arrest report should indicate that the person is a possible victim of a pickpocket so that the releasing officer may take an appropriate crime report from the victim when he has become sober and rational.

153. An officer responds to a "drunk in an accident" broadcast, and finds that the driver has been removed to a hospital. Witnesses at the scene of the collision state that the driver was very drunk.

Secure all names and addresses plus statements from witnesses who saw the person drive the car and take statements from those who can testify as to his intoxicated condition. An accident report should be completed. If the facts indicate that the suspect was drunk driving or driving under the influence of intoxicating liquor, a complaint should be secured accordingly. In many states it is legal to have a competent medical authority (doctor, physician, registered nurse or licensed laboratory technician) to take a blood sample for analysis to determine blood alcohol content as evidence of being under the influence of intoxicating liquor. This right may usually be exercised whether the person is unconscious or whether he objects to the taking of a blood sample. However, the method of taking the sample must not be brutal or shocking, but must be taken in a medically approved manner. This has been sanctioned in California by the cases of People vs. Haeussler (1953) 41 Cal. 2d 252 and People vs. Duroncelay (1957) 48 A.C. 689.

154. During an extremely busy night, an officer stops a drunken driver who lives only a block away.

Drunken driving is a serious offense, although it is generally classified as a misdemeanor. Again, appropriate tests and observations should be made to establish that the driver is under the influence of intoxicating liquor. If it is established that the driver is under the influence of liquor, he should be arrested forthwith, and appropriate reports made. If the person is released because he lives a block away, the next question is what to do if he lives two, three, or four blocks away. It would seem that an arrest should not be predicated upon distance, but rather upon the facts of the case.

155. In working the case above, the officer's partner insists upon driving the drunken driver home. Upon arrival at the person's house, he offers the officer money, and upon getting out of the car, he drops some money on the seat.

This problem should not have progressed as far as it has. If a person is drunk driving, he should be taken into custody and not be permitted to endanger his life or the lives of others. If the officer made a mistake in allowing this situation to develop, he has only himself to blame. If the money is not returned to the individual, it may be construed as bribery, which is a felony for a person to offer or receive.

156. An officer walks into a restaurant for coffee, and a woman starts talking so all can hear: "There is the dirty S.O.B. who arrested me, when I hadn't done anything. They don't have anything better to do," etc.

This woman should be checked for drunkenness. If she is drunk, she should be arrested forthwith. If she is not drunk, she should be warned that her actions may constitute a disturbance of the peace, a misdemeanor. Prior to booking her for disturbing the peace, the names and addresses of other persons who are disturbed by her actions should be obtained and incorporated in the arrest report. It may also be expedient to obtain a crime report from the person in charge of the restaurant.

157. An officer stops a drunken driver and learns that he is the editor of a metropolitan newspaper.

In making an arrest for drunk driving it is always advisable to make notes as to what the driver did, and also what was said. In this connection, an attempt should be made to administer a sobriety test. Sobriety tests vary with each department, but essentially they are designed to test balance, co-ordination, and the observable condition of the person involved, relating to his speech, demeanor, alcoholic breath (or lack of it), and condition of his eyes. Some departments also have facilities for administering an intoximeter test. In any event, the driver should be given the opportunity to take a sobriety test, and if he refuses to do so, this should be noted in the arrest report. The fact that the driver is an important person may be embarrassing but it is submitted that officers should be governed by the ethical considerations of enforcing the law fairly but impartially.

158. You are conducing an inspection and discover an officer with an alcoholic breath. What action do you take?

An alcoholic breath may denote anything from a mouthwash to intoxication; consequently, a private interview would seem appropriate. If the officer had been using a mouthwash containing alcohol, some sort of remedial action may be suggested, such as breath mints or chewing gum. On the other hand, an officer who has consumed alcohol may be performing a task in connection with his assignment such as working vice in bars. If the officer is in uniform and there is an indication of a violation of a departmental regulation, it would seem that several steps should be taken: (1) Relieve the officer of his weapon and badge; (2) Have him driven home by a superior officer; (3) Make a written report of the incident directed to the commanding officer with a copy to the chief; (4) Direct the officer to report to the office of the commanding officer the next morning. Consider the possibility of having the officer submit to an intoxication test plus a blood test.

ARREST OF PERSONS

159. The manager of a liquor store has a man in custody. He tells the officers that the arrestee had presented a check in payment of some

liquor and upon being asked for some identification, the arrestee ran out of the store but the manager caught and held him for the officers.

The manager is justified in requiring appropriate identification before cashing a check. The actions of the arrestee constitute reasonable cause for physical detention. The mere presentation of a check completes the crime of issuing or uttering a check with intent to defraud. Before booking the arrestee, the officers should question the actions of the latter because it may be possible that there is a reasonable explanation for his unusual actions. If there is no reasonable explanation, a crime report should be taken from the victim and the arrestee should be booked.

160. An officer arrests a person who is apparently drunk. The drunk states that he has diabetes, but he has liquor on his breath and his eyes are bloodshot.

Most diabetics usually carry a card identifying them as a person under a specific doctor's care. Take the arrestee to the emergency hospital or a police doctor for an examination. The officer should be especially observant for the common characteristics of drunkenness. The officer should be guided by the doctor's advice as to whether the person is drunk or suffering from a diabetic seizure. Officers should always have diabetics checked by a doctor before booking for the protection of the arrestee, and for the officer.

161. A beat officer is confronted by a merchant who excitedly points out a suspect, stating, "that man robbed me."

Emergency situations demand that the officer act upon skimpy information. Hence the officer should seize the suspect, return the suspect to the merchant for confrontation. At this point, the officer should observe the accusations made by the merchant and the admissions, if any, made by the suspect, because the actions of a suspect may amount to an actual or tacit admission against his own interest. Appropriate crime reports should be taken if the facts warrant, and the suspect should be arrested. If this is a case of petty shoplifting, a misdemeanor, the officer should inform the merchant as to his right to make an arrest. *Caution* should be exercised in such situations, because most citizens are not fully aware of the distinction between felonies and misdemeanors.

162. An officer stops a car in which there are three male occupants who are felony suspects. One suspect escapes.

Officers are generally legally justified in shooting in order to affect the arrest of a felony suspect. In most states, such action by the officer is covered under laws which state: "Homicide is justifiable when committed by public officers and those acting by their command in their aid and assistance either: (1) In obedience to any judgment of a competent court; or, (2) When necessarily committed in overcoming actual resistance to the execution of some legal process, or in the discharge of any other legal duty, or, (3) When necessarily committed in retaking felons who have been rescued or have escaped, or when necessarily committed in arresting persons charged with felony, and who are fleeing from justice or resisting arrest."

Even though shooting may be legally justified an officer should exercise extreme caution in firing his revolver. "It is better to let many guilty persons escape than to shoot one innocent person," is a frequent statement by the courts.

163. At the scene of a traffic accident the officer finds two cars involved. One of the drivers, an obviously intoxicated judge, demands the arrest of the other driver for a traffic violation.

Generally speaking a judge may order the arrest of another person by virtue of state laws which read: "A magistrate may orally order a peace officer or private person to arrest anyone committing or attempting to commit a public offense in the presence of such magistrate." If, however, the judge is obviously intoxicated, he would not be in full possession of his faculties, therefore this section would possibly not be applicable because it would not constitute a lawful order. In this case it would probably be advisable to secure the presence of a superior officer to observe the condition of the judge and to corroborate the officer's findings. It is suggested that the accident be investigated in a routine manner and that all persons be arrested for whatever violations were committed in the presence of the arresting officers.

164. An officer arrests a person upon the authority of a misdemeanor traffic warrant, and en route to the station it is discovered that the warrant is not valid.

The arrested person should be released as soon as it is discovered that the warrant is not valid. The officer should explain to the detained person why he was detained and why he is now being released, because there is nothing to be gained from trying to cover up an honest mistake. If the warrant is valid on its face, the detention would be lawful. In any event, the officer should document their activities by making complete written reports as to the time, place, witnesses, and especially length of detention.

165. An officer is informed by the dispatcher that there is a misdemeanor warrant for suspect, but after the suspect is brought to the station, the warrant cannot be found.

The officer should explain the honest mistake situation to the suspect, apologize, and return him to the place where he was arrested or to wherever the suspect wishes to be driven, if reasonable. The officer should make a complete written report of the entire incident, including the names of the persons who supplied the information, and also witnesses who may prove the element of time which the detention took. Generally, the time-stamped call sheet in communications will give the officer an accurate indication of the exact time of detention.

166. An officer serving a parking violation warrant is informed that the car was sold six months ago. The warrant was issued one month ago.

No arrest should take place in this situation, but the officer could sent a teletype to the motor vehicle department for verification. The person should be informed to make out vehicle transfer forms to be sent to the vehicle department and when the transfer of registration is confirmed, then the warrant could be returned to the court with this information. If the teletype does not confirm the transfer, then the officer should check with the alleged buyer and determine if transfer was made. Although it may be that the buyer or seller were both negligent in arranging for a transfer of title for the registered owner, it would seem that the officer should not be arbitrary in attempting to penalize one or the other for a parking violation unless the officer has some evidence as to who was in possession of the car at the time the violation occurred.

167. A warrant officer has a subpoena for a witness who is in another county.

The officer should make certain that the subpoena is endorsed by a proper judge to require the attendance of an out-of-county witness. The subpoena could then be mailed to the civil division of the other county sheriff's office for service, or the officer could drive to that location and serve the subpoena himself.

168. An officer serves a traffic warrant upon a person who states that he was just returning from court where he had paid the fine for the violation.

Generally speaking, a person who pays a fine will have a receipt in his possession. If the person cannot produce a receipt and this occurs during the daytime, the officer could phone the clerk of the court for verification. It it occurs at night, the officer should resolve any doubt in favor of the person involved. However, the officer should obtain the person's local address and place of employment, so that if the person is lying, a warrant for his arrest can be served on him at a later date.

169. In checking a suspect an officer determines that a misdemeanor warrant is on file for him but the suspect refuses to accompany the officer to the station.

This situation is covered by most state laws which read:
"An arrest by a peace officer acting under a warrant is lawful even

though the officer does not have the warrant in his possession at the time of the arrest, but if the person arrested so requests it, the warrant shall be shown to him as soon as practicable."

This means that the officer should place the person under arrest and take him to the station and pick up the warrant before booking him. The section also makes it possible for one jurisdiction to book a person even though the warrant is in the possession of another jurisdiction. In this situation, the officer could book the person before obtaining the warrant from the other jurisdiction so that it may be shown to the person arrested if he so requests. If the law requires that the officer have the warrant in his possession, the suspect should be released after the officer obtains complete identification.

170. An officer attempts to serve a warrant. He listens at the door and hears a radio and conversation. He knocks and identifies himself, after which all noise ceases and no one comes to the door.

Generally, felony warrants may be served any time of the day or night, but misdemeanor warrants must be endorsed for "night service" by the magistrate before they may be served at nighttime.

In any event, if the officer is attempting to serve a valid warrant at the proper time, then he should proceed as outlined in most state laws, which read:

"To make an arrest, a private person, if the offense be a felony, and *in all cases* a peace officer, may break open the door or window of a house in which the person to be arrested is, or in which they have reasonable grounds for believing him to be, after having demanded admittance and explained the purpose for which admittance is desired."

171. An officer has a parking violation warrant for a car registered to a husband and wife. He finds the car with both of them in it.

Since the violation is committed ostensibly by the registered owner and there are two of them, it is possible to arrest both of them. Generally speaking, however, most departments have the policy of only arresting one of them leaving it up to the persons to make a choice as to which one should be the one to be arrested.

172. An officer is in a female suspect's home, and informs her that she is under arrest, and requests that she get dressed. Instead she removes her robe and refuses to get dressed.

If a policewoman is available, she should be obtained for assistance in this situation. If a policewoman is not available, the woman should be handcuffed and an overcoat or blanket or sheet should be used to cover her, and she should be taken to the women's section of the jail. In extreme cases of hysteria, it may be advisable to call for an ambulance so that she may be strapped to a stretcher and be transported to the jail in that manner.

173. In arresting a male, it is necessary to search him.

Men should be searched immediately and thoroughly for dangerous or deadly weapons, and for those items of evidence which are incidental to the arrest. Unless unusual circumstances necessitate immediate removal of personal property from the man being arrested, no personal property except weapons or evidence should be taken from him in the field. All items of contraband should be seized and booked.

174. In making an arrest, it is necessary to use handcuffs.

When a person is arrested on a felony charge, he should always have his hands cuffed behind him. When this is impracticable, the wrist of the prisoner should be handcuffed to the wrist of the officer. A felony prisoner should be handcuffed when taken outside the confines of a jail, except when handcuffing would hamper completion of an investigation. If any arrested person gives any indication that he might become belligerent or escape, or he is difficult to handle, his hands should be handcuffed behind him in all situations, including misdemeanors. A prisoner should never be handcuffed to a fixed part of an automobile while being transported.

175. An officer requests a statement of policy regarding the transportation of prisoners.

If two officers are working together when transporting an arrestee, one officer should be seated behind the driver of the vehicle. If practicable, the prisoner should be seated in the rear seat of the vehicle. When two or more arrestees are transported together, they should be handcuffed, if possible, to each other. At least two officers should be present, if at all possible, during the entire period of transportation of female arrestees. Transporting officer in radio equipped cars should request a time check from the dispatcher and give the following:

1. Location of departure point.
2. Mileage reading upon departure.

When the officers arrive at their destination, they should give the dispatcher the:

1. Location of arrival point.
2. Mileage reading upon arrival.

The dispatcher should be notified immediately if any delay or detour is necessary during the transportation of the female arrestee.

Any female over the age of five years and under the age of eighteen years taken into custody should be dealt with insofar as possible, in the presence of a policewoman or other adult female. Whenever practicable, the female juvenile should be transported in the care and custody of a policewoman or matron. If neither is available, at least two policemen should be present during the entire period of transportation and a time and mileage check should be made, as above noted.

176. A person already arrested and in custody of an officer becomes ill or is injured.

If a person becomes ill or is injured, or complains of injury before he has been booked, the officer should:

1. Take, or have the person taken, to an emergency hospital for treatment.

2. If the illness first becomes apparent during the booking process, the jailor should be notified, so that he can take action by calling a doctor in attendance, or arranging for transportation to a hospital.

3. A copy of the hospital's record of emergency treatment should be obtained to accompany the prisoner when he is subsequently booked.

Generally, a prisoner should be considered to be in need of immediate medical attention when:

1. He is intoxicated when arrested, and does not react in a normal manner after one hour.

2. He is unconscious and not merely sleeping.

3. Any delay in medical attention or treatment might result in further complications.

177. In arresting a female, it is necessary to search her.

If a female who has been arrested must be searched, the officer may handcuff her hands behind her back and he should:

Call a policewoman or matron to the scene to conduct the search of the woman, or

Transport the woman to a policewoman or matron. However, an officer may search a woman if there are reasonable grounds to believe she is carrying a dangerous or deadly weapon. When practicable, witnesses shall be present during the search of the woman. When a woman is arrested, her purse should be taken from her immediately and searched to determine whether or not it contains dangerous or deadly weapons. When practicable, witnesses should be present during the search of the purse. If a woman shoplifter is arrested, the officer may consider the possibility of using female store detectives or employees to search the woman.

178. An officer is handed a warrant of arrest for a member of the military service who is stationed aboard a navy cruiser.

Military premises, such as bases, forts, and ships, are generally considered exclusively federal property and jurisdiction. This means that civilians and civil police have no legal right to enter such premises or ships without permission from the commanding officer of said base, fort, or ship. Therefore, permission from the commanding officer must be secured before serving a warrant of arrest (or a subpoena), on a member of the military service. It is good practice to take along an extra copy of the indictment, information, or complaint (or subpoena) upon which the warrant was issued, in case the C.O. requests a copy for the command's records.

179. An officer stops a person who has violated a city traffic ordinance. A record check reveals that he is wanted on a felony warrant. After booking the person it is found the record clerk committed an error, hence the wrong person was arrested.

The person who has been booked may be unbooked. Indeed, in this situation, the person should be released from custody immediately when it is found that an error has been made because the length of detention is very influential in ascertaining the presence or absence of good faith, and also is a determinative of the damages sustained. After releasing the person, the officer concerned should make complete written reports of the incident, and take a statement from the record clerk who committed the error. The prosecuting atorney should be notified as soon as possible regarding the incident, and his advice should be sought as to any other procedures to be followed.

180. A female about 30 years of age complains to a traffic officer that a man across the street has been trying to pick her up.

A person who persists in his attempts to "pick up" a woman is known as a "masher," is committing a disturbance of the peace, a misdemeanor. Such offensive conduct, while minor in nature, sometimes leads to kidnapping, assault, rape, and other crimes. Since this was a misdemeanor committed in the presence of the female, she should be instructed as to her rights to make a so-called "citizen's or private person's arrest," and the officer should be guided by her wishes in the matter. If the woman makes a "citizen's or private person's arrest" she should sign both the crime report and the arrest report and the arrestee should be booked to her. She should be advised as to appearing at the office of the prosecuting attorney for a complaint and for possible appearance in court as the case might go to trial. If the woman does not wish to make an arrest, officers should at least stop the suspect and make a field interrogation card on him and check him out with headquarters for a possible "want" on crimes of sex or violence before releasing him.

181. An officer arrives home from his tour of duty and his wife complains about an overly aggressive vacuum cleaner salesman who made remarks about the "filthy" house, refused to leave when first ordered to do so, and became very obnoxious at her refusal to buy.

Such actions constitute a misdemeanor, a disturbing of the peace. These actions constitute offensive conduct, and the same procedure should be followed as in the preceding question regarding the rights of the individual to make a so-called citizen's or private person's arrest.

182. A private person desires to know his rights to make an arrest.

A private person desiring to make a lawful arrest for a misdemeanor, not committed in an officer's presence, should be advised that he may (1) make a physical arrest, or (2) make a crime report, and proceed through the prosecuting attorney's office for a warrant of arrest. If a private person makes a lawful arrest and requests that an officer receive the arrestee, the officer shall do so, since this is usually a state requirement.

If a private person's arrest is, or appears to be, illegal, the arresting private person should be so advised. If the arresting person insists upon arresting the person and officers do not believe that the arrest is lawful, they should not receive the prisoner. The complaining person should be referred to the prosecuting attorney's office.

All persons involved in a private person's arrest should be advised that the officers are not making the arrest, but are merely receiving the arrested person. Officers should attempt to stay within the capacity of receiving a prisoner, rather than assisting the arrest. After receiving an arrested person, officers should:

1. Request arresting persons to accompany the officer to the station.

2. Properly fill out an arrest report. The officer's name and serial number should appear only in the narrative portion of the arrest report as "transporting officer" or as "officer receiving the arrested person."

3. Have arresting person sign the arrest report.

4. Book the arrested person to the arresting private person.

Officers should, upon demand, go to the aid of an arresting private person whose lawful arrest is being resisted.

An arrested person should not be received when the complainant is:

1. Unable to qualify as a witness.

2. Incapable of testifying to the facts of the charge.

TRAFFIC

183. When an officer attempts to write a traffic citation, the woman driver locks the door, rolls up the window, and sets the hand brake.

If persuasion fails, and the vehicle is not a traffic hazard, write down the description of the driver, secure the license number and the description of the car, secure the names and addresses of witnesses, if available, and make application for warrant of arrest. If the vehicle is a traffic hazard, secure a tow truck and tow the car to a garage where a side wing may be forced open and the driver placed under arrest, or push the car to the curb with the tow truck, take the description and secure the information as described above, and apply for a warrant of arrest.

184. An officer stops a car for running a signal light. The driver shows the officer a "courtesy card."

A courtesy card is usually defined as a small ordinary calling card on the back of which is written something to the effect, "This is my friend Joe.

Any favors shown him will be appreciated by me. Signed, Officer Knuckle-head." There is no legal basis for an officer to refrain from issuing a citation merely because a person possesses a "courtesy card." Recognition of a privileged group is both unprofessional and unethical. Citations should be issued on the basis of the situation involved and not on the basis of who knows whom. If a traffic citation is warranted it should be issued.

185. A person requests an officer to remove a car parked in front of his driveway. He also states that another car is parked completely in his driveway.

Most state vehicle laws prohibit blocking or parking in driveways and provide for the police removal of such vehicles. In such cases, the vehicle could be impounded in accordance with the appropriate sections of the law. Before an officer requests a tow truck, good public relations dictate that an attempt be made to locate the driver of the vehicle. If he will remove his vehicle, the officer may then exercise his judgment as to whether a warning or citation is in order.

186. An officer issues a citation for an illegally parked vehicle. As he leaves the scene, he observes a man come out of a store, remove the citation, read it, then rip it up and stuff it in a nearby trash container.

It would seem that the officer would have reasonable grounds to believe that the crime of malicious mischief, a misdemeanor, has been committed in his presence. Such being the case, the officer could require identification from the person, and if the officer is satisfied regarding the person's identity and that he is the legal possessor of the car, immediately release him and make a written report of the incident to accompany the original copy of the citation which he turns in at the end of the day.

187. At the scene of an accident where a person has been injured, it appears that city property may have been responsible.

Photographs of the scene should be taken, in addition to making an injury report when:
    1. The injured person indicates that a condition of city property might have caused the injury, or,
    2. There are indications that the condition of the city property might have caused the injury.
    No circumstances of the case should be mentioned to or discussed with unauthorized persons. Photographing of traffic accidents is not affected by this section, and should be carried out in accordance with standard procedure in taking photographs at the scene of serious traffic accidents.

188. An officer stops a minor traffic offender. During the course of the conversation, the defendant displays a courtesy badge. The officer also observes that the gentleman is carrying a gun under his coat.

It is not clear what is mean by a "courtesy badge" but sometimes juris-dictions will issue deputy or auxiliary badges to citizens. Sometimes the possession of such a badge will provide the necessary authority to carry a concealed weapon upon one's person. In other situations such a badge only legalizes the carrying of a concealed weapon when the person is actively on duty and in the company of a regular member of the department or force. In any event, the person should be subjected to the routine question-ing and an interrogation card be made of the incident. This is not to suggest that a "courtesy badge" gives a person any special privilege from receiving a traffic citation but on the contrary suggests that appropriate police action be taken to verify the circumstances under which the person is carrying a gun. As to the citation, it should be issued if the situation so warrants.

189. An officer observes a city-owned rubbish truck enroute to the city dump spilling part of its load.

City trucks are not immune from traffic citations. However, the practicality of the situation usually will demand that the truck driver retrace his route and pick up the spilled load.

190. A traffic officer on patrol attempts to clock a speeder. However, he discovers that the police unit is not fast enough to overtake the traffic violator.

This fact occurs too often and is frustrating to say the least. Sometimes suc-cess has been achieved by radioing the control center so that other cars can block or overtake the elusive speeder. At other times the officer may be able to get close enough to obtain the license number of the car and possibly make an application for a complaint against the registered owner. In the event the violator escapes the officer, a written report should be made of the inadequacies of the police car to apprehend said violator.

191. An officer stops a very neatly dressed woman driving a late model Cadillac for a traffic violation. She states she is in town on business from a neighboring city, and has lost her purse earlier in the day, and now is without her license, money, or identification.

The officer should check with the dispatcher for a possible stolen car, or if he is not satisfied with her story, she could be taken to the station and a teletype sent to the police of the other city, who could send a car to her residence or place of work for verification of her story. In any event, she should be checked thoroughly before being released. If the officer believes her story, then it would seem appropriate to take a lost report of her purse and contents, indicating in the report where she is staying locally.

192. While obtaining a statement from one of the drivers involved in a

traffic accident where many persons are present, one spectator continually bellows and shouts, "Don't tell them anything—see your lawyer first."

From a police standpoint, such actions may amount to an impairment of the investigation, but it does not constitute interference with an officer from a legal standpoint. In other words, there is nothing illegal about warning a person not to talk to police officers. If the noisy person takes any further action such as pushing the officer aside, then the person could be arrested for interfering with an officer. There is also a possibility of an arrest for disturbing the peace if the person is unduly loud or noisy.

193. An officer stops a man driving an old, dirty, beat-up looking car, who has committed a traffic violation. The violator's only identification is an operator's license three years expired.

This person should be checked out thoroughly before being released. If there are no traffic warrants for him, or he is not wanted for some other reason, the officer should issue a citation for the traffic violation, and for not having a valid operator's license in his possession.

194. A vehicle strikes three parked vehicles. A person is identified as the driver. He has been drinking, but is not intoxicated. One member of the driver's family was injured, but two others are all right. The driver refuses to submit to any tests or give a statement to the officers.

Unless a person is guilty of some crime, the officer has no authority to place him under arrest. Under the facts of this case, it would seem that the person should be told about complying with the state vehicle code regarding leaving his identification on the parked vehicles, and to make a report to the state department of motor vehicles. The officer should proceed to make a collision or traffic report relating all the facts therein. Every effort should be made to secure names and statements of witnesses, if any, as to the driving of the vehicle by the person concerned, but it would seem that there are not sufficient facts in this case to justify any further action than a traffic report.

195. An officer observes an official of the city government driving on a road within a park, 20 m.p.h. in excess of signs posted along the road stating "20 m.p.h. maximum."

The implication in this case is that some preference should be given to "important persons." This is not only un-American, un-democratic, and unfair but it is contrary to the dictates of good law and order. Hence, traffic violations should be handled in a fair but impartial manner, in which case the officer should exercise his own discretion regarding the issuance of a citation, as he would in any other traffic situation. If warnings are encouraged by your department, they should be used with discretion. If warning tags are not part of your departmental regulations, then it would seem that a citation would be in order. It should be understood that the law is designed to apply equally to all.

196. An officer issues a citation to a traffic violator who refuses to sign it. While en route to the station, the violator identifies himself as an attorney and now demands to sign the citation.

An attorney has no special privileges, but as a private person he should be given the same consideration as any other private person, and should be allowed to sign the citation. It is only where the person remains adamant and refuses to sign the citation at all that the arrest should be complete and the person placed in jail. The attorney should be allowed to sign the citation, and should be driven back to his car, after which complete reports should be made regarding the incident.

197. A person complains to an officer that "some boys burn rubber in front of my house" at a certain time every day.

This problem indicates that some selective enforcement should be applied to this location. This means that the police car in the area should patrol in the vicinity to observe and watch for a traffic violation. When the persons are apprehended, it would be a matter of judgment, on the part of the officer, as to whether a warning or a citation would suffice.

The complainant should be advised as to his rights to make a "citizen's" or "private person's" arrest, so that if he observes a violation in his presence, he may then take appropriate action as the situation demands.

198. An officer stops a car described in a radio broadcast as being one wanted by a neighboring police department for hit-run violation.

The hit and run may be a felony or misdemeanor. If it is a felony violation, the officer may arrest upon reasonable cause to believe the person is guilty of a felony. If it is for a misdemeanor, the hit-run is in progress, and consequently it is a misdemeanor in progress. Being a continued misdemeanor the officer could arrest for the crime being committed in his presence. In any event, the person should be stopped, placed under arrest, and the neighboring police department contacted so that they may send officers to take the person into custody, and return him to their department for booking. The action taken should be noted in the officer's log, or a complete report filed.

199. A police officer in a black and white patrol car has delivered some warrants to another city and while there he observes a person drive through a red signal.

Two courses of action seem appropriate:

1. The officer could either warn the person, or take his license number and identification, and make application for complaint in that city, or,

2. The officer could call a patrol car from that area to the location and use their citation book for writing a citation.

Departmental regulations would probably dictate which would be the recommended action.

200. A motorcycle officer apprehends a motorist travelling at a high rate of speed about fifty feet behind fire apparatus responding to a fire.

Vehicle codes usually cover this situation for which the officer could issue a citation. They generally read as follows:

"No motor vehicle, except an authorized emergency vehicle or a vehicle of a duly authorized member of a fire or police department, shall be operated within the block wherein an emergency situation responded to by any fire department vehicle exists. . . ."

"No motor vehicle except an authorized emergency vehicle or a vehicle of a duly authorized member of a fire department, shall follow within 300 feet of any vehicle of a fire department which is responding to an emergency or fire call."

201. An officer observes a fire apparatus not under red light make a turn against a posted no left turn signal.

The officer should follow the apparatus to the fire station, and after the vehicle is parked, should warn the driver that he is risking a possible civil suit by becoming involved in an accident when he is not driving as an authorized emergency vehicle. However, no citation would seem to be in order, because citizens are interested in getting the fire apparatus back to the station so that it can respond to other fire-calls, and sometimes the only way this can be done expeditiously is for the firemen to cautiously ignore such signs.

202. An officer pursues a speeding car which turns into the driveway of a service station. The driver of the car states that since he is on private property the officer cannot issue a citation. The station manager then threatens to throw the officer off his property unless he leaves immediately.

Inform the driver of the car and the station manager that you have the right to make an arrest or issue a citation under the present circumstances and that you intend to do so. Further inform the station manager that under the state law every person who resists or obstructs an officer in the discharge of his duties is guilty of a misdemeanor and that if he interferes he will be arrested. Issue the citation and if there is any interference on the part of the station manager, arrest him. If the driver of the vehicle refuses to sign the citation or to present satisfactory evidence of his identity, make a physical arrest and impound his vehicle for safe-keeping.

203. An officer in pursuit of a possible robbery suspect in a vehicle is involved in a minor traffic accident.

Two possible actions seem appropriate:

1. Proceed in pursuit of the robbery suspect and radio to communications for another car to be assigned to handle the investigation of the accident, returning to the scene of the accident as soon as possible, or;

2. Radio to communications for the assignment of another car for the chase of the robbery suspect and stop at the scene for an identification before proceeding further.

204. A uniformed officer is driving home in his private car after a tour of duty. A driver of another car makes an unsafe lane change swerving in front of the officer causing him to turn sharply to avoid a collision.

Generally, an officer is considered to be a peace officer 24 hours a day regardless of whether or not he is on duty. This means that the officer could issue a citation if he has one available. If not, the officer could take the license number and description of the driver and make an application for complaint for the unsafe lane change. The above does not preclude the officer from stopping the driver and issuing a warning regarding the unsafe lane change. Discretion will indicate whether a police action should be taken by an off-duty officer in such situations.

205. An officer is directing traffic at a busy intersection downtown. An east bound vehicle goes through the intersection against the red signal, causing the north bound traffic to stop to avoid a collision.

Under these facts, there seems to be no good reason for not issuing a traffic citation. If, however, the stopping of the vehicle for the period of time necessary to issue a citation would unduly hamper the flow of traffic, the officer could take the vehicle license number, driver's license number, description, and release the driver after telling him that an application for a complaint will be sought for the violation. The main duty of an officer when directing traffic is to facilitate the flow of traffic; therefore, he should not normally become involved in enforcement activities.

206. A patrol officer stops the driver of a car after observing him drive through an intersection without stopping for the boulevard stop sign. The driver complains that bushes partially hid the stop sign, and he didn't see it until too late to stop.

In practically all traffic violation cases, it is not necessary to prove that there was any intent on the part of the persons concerned to violate the law. But in the interest of justice, the officer should verify the claim and if what the driver says is true, no citation should be written, but instead, a written report should be made and sent through departmental channels so that the proper department may then take appropriate action to remove the obstruction. Meanwhile, it may be possible that the officer could tear off branches from the bushes in order to prevent accidents from occurring at the location.

207. An officer begins to write a parking violation citation on a vehicle illegally parked in a red zone. The driver of the vehicle approaches and complains that the paint is partially obliterated.

A citation should not be issued if at the time of the violation, any required official sign or marking is not in place and sufficiently legible and visible to be seen by an ordinarily observant person. The officer should make a written report to his immediate superior and when approved the report should be forwarded through channels to the department concerned. If the officer determines that the zone is sufficiently marked as to be seen by a normally observant person, the citation then may be issued.

208. An officer stops a driver of a car for a minor traffic violation and decides to merely warn him without writing a citation. As the officer leaves, the driver demands his name, serial number, and division of assignment.

The officer should comply with his request, because this is a reasonable request. If the officer is suspicious of the motives of the person concerned, he should make a record of the time, place, etc., and enter it in his personal notebook. Experience indicates that such information is requested for the purpose of commendations by citizens.

209. An officer on patrol stops an erratic driver. It is established that the driver is involuntarily under the influence of paint fumes, and he insists on driving while in this condition.

The driver should be examined by a doctor at the emergency hospital for possible driving while under the influence of narcotic drugs. Although there is no violation for being under the influence of insecticide or paint fumes as such, it may be that there is some state law which covers such conditions. If it is determined that no law exists covering such situations, the driver should be cautioned and released. A full report of the incident, including the doctor's statement, should be made.

210. A vehicle runs into a house due to negligent driving. The house owner insists on holding the vehicle as a lien against the damage to his house.

Generally speaking, a person is not legally entitled to seize property as security for damages. The officer should advise the person that his remedy is to secure an attorney for a possible civil suit for damages. If the owner of the vehicle attempts to drive it away, and is restrained, the person causing the restraint could be arrested for disturbing the peace. A crime report should be taken from the owner of the vehicle. If no arrest is made, a report of the automobile accident should be made in the usual manner.

211. An officer stops a truck for a minor traffic violation. The officer finds that there is an outstanding $100 traffic warrant for the driver. The truck is loaded with perishables, and headed for another state.

The driver could be immediately arrested under the traffic warrant and be admitted to bail, in which case the perishables would probably not stand longer than an hour or two on the street. If, for some reason, the perishables might suffer, the truck or its contents could be impounded at either an ice company or some similar place in the area. Most ice companies have provisions for cold storage of large quantities of perishables which they keep for a reasonable length of time before selling and applying the proceeds to the storage costs. If the driver does not have sufficient money to post bail, it may be possible to contact the owner of the truck or company, so that someone else can post bail without unnecessary delay, or the truck could be released to another authorized driver. Another solution would be to serve the warrant at a later date because there is no crime committed if the officer does not serve the warrant under the facts of this case.

212. A citizen calls concerning a strange automobile which has been parked in front of his residence with no evident ownership for two days. Investigation indicates that the automobile is not stolen.

A report should be made of the incident, so that if a stolen report is made at a later date, the car could be readily located. The officers could also canvass the neighborhood on both sides of the street in an attempt to locate the owner or legal possessor of the car. Unless there is some city or county ordinance authorizing impounding a vehicle under such conditions, no other action seems necessary other than indicated. That department of the state government which handles the registration of motor vehicles could be called regarding the ownership of the vehicle. The owner could then be notified by telephone or letter.

213. An officer observes an ambulance with red light and siren, occupied by a patient, being driven in excess of 65 m.p.h. during heavy traffic conditions.

Under most state laws, ambulances are emergency vehicles, but they must be driven with due regard for the safety of all persons using the highway. The officer should check the speed of the vehicle, and follow it to its destination. It may be that an extreme emergency may have motivated the driver to drive as he did. If the facts warrant a citation, one should be written, but generally speaking, a warning will suffice. If the officer is in doubt if a citation should be issued, he can proceed by making application for complaint at a later time. One thing seems obvious: the ambulance should not be stopped unless there is an absolute certainty that the continued driving of same will result in catastrophe. If continued incidents of excessive speed are noted by officers, then it would seem that the concerned public agency or private owner should be warned in writing.

214. At the scene of a serious traffic accident an officer calls for an ambulance and is informed that none is available for over an hour. One of the injured persons requests to be taken to a hospital in the police vehicle.

Many state vehicle codes now provide that a police vehicle may be used for an ambulance. Generally, such laws state that "any peace officer may transport or arrange for the transportation of any person injured in an accident upon any highway to a physician and surgeon or hospital, if the injured person does not object to such transportation. Any officer exercising ordinary care and precaution shall not be liable for any damages due to any further injury or for any medical, ambulance, or hospital bills incurred in behalf of the injured party." (From California Vehicle Code, Section 20,016.)

215. A traffic officer observes a pedestrian erase several "overtime parking" tire marks from vehicles which the officer has just marked.

This is no crime. It would take a special city or county ordinance to specifically prohibit such actions before an arrest could be made. The officer should resort to some other method than the marking of tires to determine if in fact a violation has occurred. One enterprising officer placed peanuts under one of the wheels of a suspected automobile.

216. An officer stops a vehicle which was going 95 m.p.h. on a highway. The driver says he is going to a hospital with a passenger who is choking.

Departmental regulations will dictate whether or not you may act as escort in such situations. The officer should verify the facts, advise the driver to go slower, or if department regulations permit, escort the vehicle to the hospital with your red light and siren operating.

217. An officer is called by a citizen who points out a house trailer parked next to a fire hydrant. The trailer is not attached to a motor vehicle.

The parking of vehicles next to a fire hydrant is a misdemeanor. In such cases the officer should attempt to locate the owner of the trailer and have him move it, or failing in this, he can enforce the local regulation.

218. In attempting to cite a person for a traffic violation, the officer determines that the violator is a deaf-mute and is unable to understand or communicate.

Most deaf-mutes are able to understand by reading lips and are able to communicate their thoughts by writing. If this person is not able to read lips or is unable to write, the officer could attempt to convey his meaning by displaying his own driver's license and other identification. As a last resort the officer could release the driver and proceed by application for complaint after securing a good description of the driver, and the license number of the car.

219. An officer attempts to stop a traffic violator with a red light and a siren. The person refuses to stop.

Officers chasing a violator should radio the dispatcher, giving him the make of the car, the license number if they have it, color of the car, and direction of travel. Radio contact should be kept with the dispatcher, keeping him informed of the direction of travel, in order to set up possible road blocks. A running check should be made on the car to find out if it is possibly stolen, or the occupant wanted for a felony. If the answer is to the affirmative, the suspects should be approached as in any other felony case.

220. An officer is chasing a driver in a stolen car, who might possibly be a juvenile. He is unable to overtake him, but is within shooting distance.

The general rule is to the effect that "when in doubt, don't shoot." In this situation it would seem more appropriate to radio for assistance and continue the chase. Experience has shown that in a prolonged chase the escapee consistently crashed his car or was intercepted by converging police units.

221. An officer observes a person taking photographs at the scene of an accident. The photographer states that he is a newspaperman and used the radio in his car to learn of such calls. He is unable to identify himself as a reporter of any kind.

Recently the Los Angeles, California, City Ordinance relating to prohibiting listening to police calls was declared unconstitutional. Unless there is a constitutional ordinance prohibiting such action in your jurisdiction, it is suggested that the officer refrain from taking any action. It is not illegal to take pictures at the scene of accidents on public streets, so long as a person photographing does not interfere with traffic or with police activities at the scene. If there is a blocking of traffic or police interference, the person may be arrested.

222. A woman jaywalker refuses to identify herself.

This person is possibly guilty of violating a section of the state vehicle code which usually reads as follows: "Between adjacent intersections controlled by traffic control signal devices or by police officers, pedestrians shall not cross the roadway at any place except in a crosswalk."

Generally, warnings will suffice in such situations. If the officer is convinced that a warning would not have any corrective effect, then an arrest is justified.

If the person refuses to identify himself, then the officer has no choice but to arrest the person.

223. A person is arrested for drunk driving and he demands that his car not be impounded.

Generally, the condition of such person will preclude sound judgment, hence the car should be impounded. If his wife, or other responsible person is present, it may be possible that such person could take the car. Officers should be careful to verify the identification of the person to whom the car is released. Consult local laws regarding authority to impound.

224. An officer stops two sixteen-year-old boys in an unmarked panel truck for a minor traffic violation. The officer observes two bottles of liquor with seals unbroken inside the truck. They state that they are employed by Jones Market and are delivering the liquor to a customer.

The officer should write the citation and make a complete report for follow up action by the juvenile officer. The vice officer should be alerted for possible Alcoholic Beverage Control violations by the liquor store owner.

225. An officer answers a "meet the sergeant" call and is directed to arrest a person seated in a parked car for drunk driving.

A peace officer may arrest a person when there is reasonable cause for believing that a misdemeanor is being committed in his presence. One of the elements of drunk driving is that the person was seen driving. If the sergeant witnessed the driving, the sergeant should make the arrest. However, it is sometimes the practice for sergeants to request officers to serve as transporting officers. In such a situation the officers should transport the drunk driver to the jail and indicate in the arrest and booking report that the sergeant is the arresting officer. The report covering the field arrest should be made by the sergeant, and if assisted by another officer, said officer should also file a report.

226. After an officer writes a traffic citation, the driver refuses to sign it.

The general rule is that the person should be allowed to sign the citation up to the time that he is actually placed in jail. Prior to the jailing of the person, it should be explained to the person that he is merely promising to appear in court, and the signing of the citation is not an admission of guilt. The officer should assume a professional attitude of being courteous, impartial, and of being firm and fair in his duty of upholding the law. If the person refuses to accept the citation, it would appear that the officer would have no choice but to arrest and jail the person.

227. An officer stops a mail truck because of erratic driving. The driver, a postal employee, is drunk.

The driver should be arrested for drunk driving, a misdemeanor. Since the officer is responsible for taking custody of the mail truck and its contents, the postal superintendent should be contacted immediately and the truck guarded pending the arrival of said superintendent, or other supervisor. After the truck and its contents have been turned over to the custody of the postal personnel, proceed with the booking of the driver and the making of reports in the usual manner.

228. An officer pursues a speeding car and finally forces it to the curb. The driver jumps out and runs into a house before the officers can apprehend him.

An attempt to elude an officer makes the person subject to a physical arrest, and in this situation the officer may break into the house. Most state laws provide that: "To make an arrest, a private person, if the offense be a felony, and in all cases a peace officer may break open the door or window of the house in which the person to be arrested is, or in which they have reasonable grounds for believing him to be, after having demanded admittance and explained the purpose for which admittance is desired." If an officer decides that the situation does not merit a physical arrest, he may make an application to the prosecuting attorney or the court for the issuance of a warrant of arrest, so that the violator may be arrested under more convenient circumstances.

229. A person is involved in a collision and is removed to a hospital before the arrival of an officer. A partially filled whisky bottle is found in his car and several people state that the driver had been drinking. At the hospital the doctor refuses to permit the officer to see the person.

Ask the doctor for the driver's name, address, and driver's license and for an opinion as to whether subject had been drinking and if he will take a blood sample. Request the doctor to notify you when the patient is to be released. If the welfare of the patient will not suffer by an interview, then advise the doctor that his actions may constitute interfering with an officer, and either arrest him or the doctor, or make application for complaint if the situation so demands. The officer may consider taking the following actions against the alleged driver: (1) Reasonable to assume violation of drunk driving, a misdemeanor. (2) Arrange for photographs of scene and take notes on the circumstances. (3) Preserve the whisky bottle and contents as evidence. (4) Identify and take statements from witnesses as to driver's state of intoxication. (5) Call a tow truck and impound the vehicle for safekeeping. (6) Obtain names of the ambulance driver, doctor and members of the staff at the hospital and get statements. (7) No legal grounds for seeing the driver without first obtaining a warrant.

230. An officer stops a borderline traffic violator for a warning. The vio-

lator immediately takes the offensive, denies the violation and suggests the officer spend more time catching criminals, etc.

If an officer stops a traffic violator for a warning it should never turn into a ticket. The officer should have fortified himself with the traffic accident statistics, such as amount of economic loss during the past year, or number of deaths, and particularly at that location. In this manner the officer will be more likely to present valid arguments in support of the time he is spending enforcing traffic violations. Instead of the officer taking a defensive stand this particular violator should serve as a challenge for the officer to point out the necessity for good selective traffic enforcement. However, the officer should not spend a great deal of time but should present his side of the argument and then take a courteous departure.

231. An officer on "stakeout" duty for narcotics observes an auto theft. He has no radio contact. What is his course of action?

Although a narcotic stakeout is important, still this situation indicates that grand theft auto, a felony, is being committed in the presence of the officer. It would seem that the officer's only course of action is to follow the auto thief and arrest him at some distance from the stakeout. In this way he has made a felony arrest and at the same time has possibly preserved the stakeout area for further stakeouts. After arresting the grand theft auto suspect the officer could call for other officers to take over and make the appropriate bookings and impounding of the stolen vehicle plus appropriate written reports so that he could return to the scene of the narcotics stakeout. However, he should contact his superior regarding the events which took place and the time which has elapsed so that some judgment can be made as to whether or not the narcotics stakeout should be continued.

232. An officer arrests a person for speeding just a few yards from his own home and issues a citation. The person refuses to sign and the sergeant rolls by and orders the officer to release the violator from custody.

Generally speaking a person who refuses to sign a citation should be placed under arrest and booked. Under California law the authority for such an arrest is covered thusly: "Whenever any person is arrested for any violation of this code, not declared herein to be a felony, the arrested person shall be taken without unnecessary delay before a magistrate within the county in which the offense charge is alleged to have been committed and who has jurisdiction of such offense and is nearest or most accessible with reference to the place where the arrest is made or, if the magistrate is not available before his clerk or (1) the officer in charge of a jail wherein the person arrested could be held in custody upon the charge for which he was arrested as provided in Section 1269b of the Penal Code, in any of the following cases: . . . (b) When the person arrested refuses to give his written promise to appear in court."

However, there is nothing in the law that states that some other action might not be appropriate. This means that if the sergeant wants the officer to release the violator from custody such an order may be following your departmental policy. In such a case it would be appropriate to make written reports and proceed by application for complaint against the violator.

233. An officer investigating a traffic accident asks the sergeant to take certain pictures of the vehicles involved but he refuses or passes it off as being unnecessary.

Generally speaking the officer charged with the investigation is personally responsible for taking all the necessary steps and procedures. This means that if the officer believes that photos should be taken of the vehicles or scene he should use every means available to secure such photographs, even to the extent of calling the superior of both himself and the sergeant involved. Prior thereto however, it would seem that some discussion should be had with the sergeant as to his reasons for not considering the photographs important. In all questions of judgment people will differ, hence some efforts should be made towards reaching a reasonable conclusion instead of an arbitrary decision. If the officer is convinced the sergeant is correct he could note this fact in the report made of the accident.

234. An officer at the scene of a fire sees an automobile driven over the fire hose in the street.

This is a violation under most state vehicle codes. They generally read as follows:

"No person shall drive or propel any vehicle or conveyance upon, over or across, or in any manner damage any fire hose or chemical hose used by or under the supervision and control of any organized fire department. However, any vehicle may cross such hose, provided suitable jumpers or other appliances are installed to protect such hose."

The officer may proceed by warning the driver, or by issuing a citation, depending upon the situation.

235. A store owner whose store is on fire doesn't heed the warning of a police officer to keep his car out of the fire area, runs over the fire hose, parks his car in front of his store and forces his way in against order of firemen.

As in the last problem, a person driving his car over the hose would probably be in violation of the code. The vehicle code will generally read something similar to:

"Every person is guilty of a misdemeanor who,

"1. Disobeys the lawful orders of any public officer or fireman.

"2. Offers any resistance to or interference with the lawful efforts of any fireman or company of firemen to extinguish the fire.

"3. Engages in any disorderly conduct calculated to prevent the fire from being extinguished.

"4. Forbids, prevents, or dissuades others from assisting to extinguish the fire."

It would seem that before an arrest is made that the person should be interrogated as to his reasons for wanting to enter the building.

236. A motorcycle officer directing traffic at a fire is nearly run down by a person who believes that it is his store that is burning.

This is considered an occupational hazard, and unless some flagrant violation has occurred, the officer should merely warn the person regarding driving fast. If some violations have occurred, it would seem that a citation may be in order, but the officer should be guided by facts and not emotions.

237. A citizen approaches a traffic officer and asks the location of a street within the city limits. The officer is uncertain of its location.

It is not unusual for an officer to be uncertain as to the location of streets, places, buildings, or public events, especially in large cities. The officer should consult his street guide, or if he has none, should telephone headquarters for assistance. A citizen does not expect an officer to know everything, but he does expect an officer to try to help him, in solving legitimate problems. This is one of those cases which could do both the officer and the department immeasurable good by helping the citizen as much as possible.

238. An officer observes two vehicles racing at excessive speed. When attempting to stop both vehicles, only one does so—the other turns off onto a side street and disappears.

Attempting to evade an arrest by a peace officer or a traffic officer is usually a misdemeanor under most state vehicle codes, for which a physical arrest can be made. A radio broadcast should be made immediately on the escaping vehicle, giving a description and the direction taken, for interception by other police units.

When the person is apprehended, he should be either arrested and jailed, or issued a traffic citation, depending upon departmental policy.

239. A motorist complains that a businessman has placed a sign in front of his establishment reading: "No Parking. This Space Is Reserved For Customers."

If the sign is located upon private property, there would be no violation. But the posting or maintaining such a sign upon public property usually constitutes a misdemeanor under most city or county ordinances. In some situations it may violate the State Vehicle or Traffic Code as imitating or purporting to be an official traffic control sign.

No physical arrest should be made without a warrant unless the offense was committed in the presence of the officer. Instead, the better practice would seem to consist of two steps:

1. Warn the violator that he should remove the sign or a warrant for his arrest may be issued, or

2. Make application for a warrant by contacting the office of the prosecuting attorney. If the facts justify a prosecution, the prosecutor will authorize it.

240. An officer observes a motor vehicle with the front license plate differing from that on the rear of the vehicle.

Such a vehicle must be approached with the idea that it may be a stolen car, or that it is being driven by a burglar, robber, or other felon. Exercising caution, the general police procedures should be followed in interrogating the driver regarding the two different license plates. An insufficient or unsatisfactory explanation would demand that the driver and the auto be taken to headquarters, where a more detailed inquiry may be conducted.

241. A motorist, upon being stopped for a minor traffic violation, informs the officer that "he is leaving the state and won't return so it is useless to issue him a ticket."

The comment that "he is leaving the state" should not influence the officer as to whether or not a ticket (citation) should be issued. If the violation is such that a ticket should be written, the officer should proceed to do so. On the other hand, if the situation calls for a mere warning no citation need be written.

In a few states the vehicle laws provide that an officer may take the violator directly to court or to a clerk to post bail. The officer should proceed as authorized by law.

242. An officer stops a vehicle for a traffic violation and decides to search the vehicle because the driver is argumentative and antagonistic.

Generally, an automobile may be searched without a warrant where the officer has reasonable cause to believe it is carrying contraband or where he has reasonable cause to physically arrest an occupant of an automobile and take him into custody. But a search made as an incident to a lawful arrest must be related to the crime for which the arrest was made; for example, where an arrest is made for a traffic offense, such as double parking, a search made of the back seat of the car would not be related to the offense for which the driver was arrested (cited for).

243. At the scene of a traffic accident the officer observes debris in the street, consisting of broken glass, dirt, and parts of broken bumpers.

Generally, state vehicle laws provide that "any person who drops, or permits to be dropped or thrown upon any highway any destructive or injurious material shall immediately remove the same or cause the same to be removed," a violation of which would constitute a misdemeanor. It would seem appropriate to inform the drivers concerned regarding the possibility of violating the law unless the debris was removed from the street. Failure to comply should call for the issuance of a traffic citation or an arrest. If, however, the parties are so incapacitated as to preclude compliance with such a regulation, then the officer should assume the responsibility to clear the street of the dangerous material.

244. An officer on patrol observes a vehicle being driven 27 m.p.h. in a posted 25 m.p.h. zone, and stops the driver for speeding.

Most departments have a policy of permitting a driver to exceed the speed limit of a posted zone by a specified amount. This is known as a "speed tolerance" and is usually adopted to compensate for mechanical and human error, and is not designed to provide a driver with an implied consent to exceed the established speed limit. In such cases, if such a "speed tolerance" is in effect the violator should be cited for driving in excess of the permissible speed and should be cited for the actual estimated or clocked speed. The same tolerance policy usually applies to the enforcement of weight and size regulations of trucks and vehicles.

245. An officer clocks a vehicle being driven at 75 m.p.h. in a 25 m.p.h. zone. When stopped, the driver claims that he is a doctor on the way to deliver a baby. There is a woman in the car, not pregnant.

Identification should be demanded to verify the driver's story about being a doctor. Next, the officer should ask for the address of the place where the baby is to be delivered. If the address and direction in which the vehicle is proceeding indicates that the driver is telling the truth, he may be released. On the other hand, if there is any doubt as to the veracity of the driver, the officer may follow him to his destination. Under some state laws it is legal to escort by using a red light and siren where emergency situations exist. If the story proves to be untrue, the officer should cite for all violations committed and send the person to court. A complete written report should be made of the incident for departmental records and for use in court.

246. An officer at a downtown intersection stops a driver for turning against a no left turn sign. A crowd gathers and the driver, at first, refuses to display his operator's license. When he does, it turns out that he is an official, and he mentions that he is in a great hurry.

No person should be detained an unreasonable length of time for the issuance of a traffic citation or ticket. When the delay is caused by the violator, the officer should mention that the sooner the violator cooperates by displaying his driver's license, the quicker the citation may be completed, and the driver can be on his way. Such situations as this demand that the officer exercise his usual tact and decorum while issuing the ticket.

It is suggested that the time it took to issue the citation be noted upon the ticket, including the reason therefor, where more than 10 minutes has elapsed.

247. An officer stops a person for speeding near the person's residence. After handing the officer a driver's license, the person runs into the house and locks the door.

Most jurisdictions authorize an officer to pursue the violator to break and enter if entry is barred. If the officer decides to pursue this course of action he should first secure assistance to prevent an escape from the rear or side exits. He should then knock on the door and demand admittance before making a forced entry, because the person may have a reasonable explanation for running into the house, such as illness or other emergency.

When in doubt, the officer could defer action by making an application for the issuance of a warrant of arrest, which could be served at a more convenient time. The warrant should be for the original violation and for the crime of evading arrest.

248. An automobile strikes a pedestrian who sustains minor injuries. There is doubt the driver has knowledge, but while you are at the scene, he drives by again and is pointed out by witnesses. When he is stopped, he identifies himself as a retired official.

Part of the corpus delicti of hit and run is that the person has knowledge that his car is involved. This may be shown by the fact that the person saw what happened, and then drove away, or by the magnitude of the collision which would cause sufficient damage that it could be said that a reasonable person should have known that his car was involved. Since there is doubt in this case, as to whether there is an actual hit and run, it would probably not be advisable to make a physical arrest, but to proceed by application for complaint to the prosecuting attorney after having taken appropriate traffic accident reports.

249. An officer answers a call to investigate an extensive property damage traffic accident. One driver involved is an old friend. He rushes over, shakes your hand, and shouts, "Hello old pal, am I glad to see you." This remark is overheard by the other driver and several citizens.

An officer investigating the accident should proceed to make the required reports and secure the names of as many witnesses as possible. The routine handling of a case will do much to alleviate the apprehension some persons must engender because of the remarks of the individual in this situation. It is not unusual for officers to be acquainted with parties involved in accidents or crimes. This is just another instance of where the assumption of a professional attitude by an officer will inspire confidence in the spectators.

250. An officer sees a driver who fails to yield the right of way to an ambulance, when the ambulance is using siren and red lights.

If the ambulance has its lights and siren on, it then qualifies as an emergency vehicle, to which other persons must yield the right of way. In this situation, the officer should pull the driver over and write a citation. (In some states, a loud horn instead of a siren is used.)

251. A funeral procession is proceeding through an intersection against a stop signal and is struck by a vehicle.

Funeral processions generally have no legal right to proceed against a stop signal. This is a delicate situation for which no citations are usually given. Appropriate traffic reports should be taken and the driver advised that he should see an attorney. Application should be made to the prosecuting attorney for a possible issuance of a complaint against the driver in the funeral procession for running a signal.

252. An officer is given the license number of a hit and run driver, in a misdemeanor accident. After checking the vehicle records, the officer goes to the home of the suspect. Upon arrival, and before informing the suspect of the nature of the visit, the officer is informed by the suspect that he is an "influential citizen." The suspect then denies all charges after being apprised of them.

Since this is a misdemeanor and not committed in the presence of the officer, no physical arrest may be made. The officer should proceed to examine the vehicle of the suspect, and then make appropriate reports and an application for complaint for hit and run, if the facts reveal that a crime has been committed. If the suspect refuses to permit the officer to see the vehicle, the officer should arrange for a stakeout on the suspect's house and garage until a search warrant is obtained. After the officer is allowed to inspect the vehicle, any evidence of damage that appears should be photographed and taken in for evidence.

253. A motorcycle rider is injured in a traffic accident. Prior to removal to the emergency hospital, he requests officers not to impound his motorcycle, because he wants to pick it up later.

A motorcycle does not take up much space, hence it could hardly be classified as a traffic hazard under most circumstances. It would seem proper for the officer to comply with the request of the rider, even to the extent of wheeling it to a parking lot or service station with the request that it be kept for safekeeping as the rider so indicates.

254. An officer driving to court in his own car is involved in a minor traffic accident. The other party will only show a business card as identification, and is belligerent. There are no license plates on his car. Court will convene in 20 minutes, and it is a felony case in which the officer is the principal witness.

In this situation, it may be possible to telephone for another officer to handle the investigation. If this is not feasible, it may be possible to phone the court and explain the situation, and ask that the trial be delayed for an hour or so in order that a check of the car may be made, to determine if it could possibly be stolen. If the officer is unable to obtain assistance, and the court will not grant an extension of time, the officer should telephone the radio dispatcher with a request that other officers in the area be on the lookout for the described car without plates as being a possible grand theft auto, and then proceed to court.

A failure to appear in court in time may result in being held in contempt of court, a misdemeanor, as well as dismissal of the case.

255. An officer writes 20 or 30 citations per month, but his partner writes about 80, and many of them seem borderline.

Traffic tickets are not popular with the public, and borderline tickets should never be issued. Before an officer criticizes his partner, it would seem advisable to consult with a superior regarding any of the situations in which a partner issued a citation and it seemed borderline. If the superior agrees that under the factual situations presented the citation is borderline, then some constructive criticism to the partner should follow. Since criticism by anyone is not easily accepted, the utmost discretion should be exercised in bringing about a correction of the situation. The supervisor could announce at roll call that quality and not quantity is the desired end when issuing citations, but no names should be mentioned in the presence of other officers, causing the officer in question undue embarrassment.

256. An officer observes a person walking a half block ahead, dropping pennies in all expired parking meters.

Unless there is some specific ordinance covering this situation, it would seem that the person is performing legally. There is no law against giving money away. Also, it would *not* seem to come within the definition of interfering with an officer. Sometimes, parking limitation signs are present which limit the length of time a person may park his car, even though the parking meter does not register a violation. The person dropping pennies in the meters is not committing a law violation, but the vehicles may still be parked overtime.

257. While investigating an accident, an officer directs a driver not to make a legal right hand turn, which the driver ignores.

This situation is usually covered by a state's vehicle code. If the officer has good reason for giving such a direction or order, then it would seem that the wrongdoer should be stopped for possible issuance of a citation. Of course, the severity of the accident under investigation might prevent an officer from turning aside for a minor traffic infraction. It is always possible to merely note the license number of the car concerned and make an application for complaint against the registered owner thereof, if the situation seems to warrant such action.

258. A citizen complains that too many trucks park in front of his house.

There are few state laws covering the parking of trucks in this situation. If there is an existing city or county ordinance regulating such parking, then the appropriate action would be under the appropriate ordinance section. Some departments have warnings or complaint tags which inform the person that their vehicle is causing complaints or violating some law. It has been found that warnings for minor violations or infractions of the law are effective.

259. At the scene of a traffic accident, officers find many injured persons. Some of the bystanders tell the officers to render first aid.

Very few police agencies provide for training in first aid. As a consequence of this, and the lack of laws covering the subject, officers are neither required nor expected to render first aid to an injured person. The most that can be said with any degree of certainty is that the officers should render to any injured person "reasonable assistance," including the carrying of such person to a physician, surgeon or hospital for medical or surgical treatment if it is apparent that treatment is necessary or if such carrying is requested by the injured person. If the injured person is unconscious, and it appears that he may be seriously injured, it would seem that the person should be transported to the hospital or doctor on a stretcher rather than in the rear seat of a police vehicle. Pending arrival of the ambulance, the officer may protect the person from further injury, apply a compress to open bleeding wounds, and make the person as comfortable as possible. First aid should be rendered only by those trained in first aid.

260. In proceeding to an emergency call, an officer's police car scrapes a fender of a parked car.

Although police cars are not exempt from provisions of a vehicle code relating to hit and run, it would seem that the seriousness of the emergency call would dictate the appropriate action to be taken in this instance. If the call is of such serious consequence that it should take precedence over stopping and finding the owner of the parked car, it would seem that the police car should proceed to answer the emergency call. On the way to the call, the officer could radio communications regarding the incident so that another car could be sent to the scene of the collision, and appropriate action could be taken in compliance with the provisions of the vehicle code.

If the emergency call isn't of too serious nature, the officer could stop and fulfill the provisions of the vehicle code and radio communications that another car be dispatched to answer the emergency call.

VICE AND NARCOTICS

261. Officers arrest a narcotic addict for possession of marijuana, and upon taking the suspect to the detectives, they are told that he is a valuable informer.

Under most state laws, it is a felony to possess marijuana. However, there is an exception to the law pertaining to the possession of narcotics under most state laws, similar to the California Health and Safety Code, Section 11710, which says: "All duly authorized peace officers while investigating violations of this division in performance of their official duties, and ANY PERSON working under their immediate supervision or instruction or direction, are IMMUNE from prosecution under this division." If the addict is actually working for the detectives, he should be turned over to the detectives. If he is not within the purvue of the exception, he should be arrested for the felony of possession of narcotics, and the marijuana should be retained as evidence in the usual manner.

262. A desk officer receives a call from a wife who complains that her husband is in a room of a certain hotel with another woman.

Generally speaking, this is a vice problem. The vice officer in handling such a problem would want to know whether or not this woman is a prostitute, and whether or not the husband is living with the woman as husband and wife. Under the criminal adultery laws of most states a married person must live with another person before the action will constitute adultery, a misdemeanor. Mere "shacking up" or occasional acts of intercourse will not constitute criminal adultery in most states. If the woman is a prostitute, she and the husband may be in violation of some city or county ordinances relating to resorting to a room or place for the purpose of sexual intercourse. In any event, all information should be obtained and relayed to the vice officer for this investigation. It should be emphasized, however, that the police department does not gather evidence for divorce purposes.

263. An officer receives a complaint from a citizen that a church is conducting a bingo and gambling party. This fact is verified by the officer.

Churches are not exempt from the state, county, or city laws prohibiting gambling. However, discretion would seem to indicate that a warning might suffice if the action is stopped immediately. At this point, departmental policy would dictate whether or not the gambling equipment should be seized and booked as evidence and a criminal complaint sought.

264. A vice officer enters a business office to interview a victim and observes an employee sitting at a phone taking bookmaking action.

Bookmaking is a felony under most state laws, and a failure to enforce the law on the part of the observing officer is a misdemeanor in some states. The evidence should be seized, the suspect arrested, and the booking should be made in the usual manner. However, if the officer is of the opinion that others may be involved in this bookmaking action, the officer could make mental notes of the situation and make a complete written report to his superior officer, so that a complete investigation of the situation could be made to stop any sort of a "ring" which may be operating.

265. A narcotics officer stops a suspected narcotics peddler on the street, and accuses him of having narcotics in his possession. The suspect puts his hands up and states, "go ahead and search me." The officer searches the suspect and finds two Benzedrine® tablets in his trouser cuff.

The general rule is that persons who are arrested on suspicion of possession of narcotics should be booked for a felony under a state narcotics act, and any tablets seized should be turned over to the scientific investigation laboratory for analysis. Usually the possession of Benzedrine tablets without a prescription is a misdemeanor. In this case, if the officer is qualified to determine that the tablets are in fact Benzedrine, the arrest should be made under the law covering the unauthorized possession of non-narcotic drugs.

266. An officer in an attempt to serve a traffic violation warrant on a suspect smells the odor of marijuana when the suspect opens the door of his apartment.

A traffic warrant will not justify a felony search. However, the smell of marijuana smoke will justify a felony arrest and a search for the narcotic. Hence, the officer should place the suspect under arrest and conduct a thorough search of the premises. It is assumed that the officer in this situation is sufficiently qualified to testify as to the smell of marijuana smoke.

267. A vice officer is told by a known prostitute the following: "I can give you a lot of information on the other girls if you will forget that I'm in the business."

Legally, the officer has no authority to promise any person an immunity from arrest. It is the general practice, however, to use prostitutes as informants. If it is decided that this person would make a good informer, such facts should be reported to one's superior officer for permission to use her. It is considered good police work to use every possible legal means to catch violators.

The facts here would indicate that the officer will have acquired a good informer, providing the conditions are met.

268. Two vice officers working under cover on an important assignment must avoid being "made" as policemen or their past work will be wasted and the suspects will probably get away. While in a bar, the officers are challenged by two belligerent drunks who "swing" on the officers.

Make a tactical withdrawal, or if necessary, exercise the right of self defense. If other officers arrive at the scene, do not identify self as a police officer, but submit to an arrest—after arrival at the jail notify (discreetly) the booking officers of your status and assignment. At this point, it may be advantageous to proceed with the booking, fingerprinting, and mugging, and have another officer arrange for a "release" or "bail" by some "friend." (This is not an official bail bond, but only a pretended one, calculated to impress the uninformed.) The main objective is to preserve the anonymity of the vice officers.

269. A motel owner stops a motorcycle officer and complains that a person in one of his units, registered as a single, just took a girl in and thinks they are having intercourse.

Mere sexual intercourse is no crime under most state laws. However, some city and county ordinances exist which prevent two persons, not married to each other, from resorting to any place for the purpose of having sexual intercourse. If such exists, a vice officer or plainclothes officer should be called for a proper investigation. It must be remembered that a specific intent to perform sexual intercourse is part of the corpus delicti in most ordinances, therefore, the time element is extremely important. This means if there has been a time lapse between entering the room and the act itself, it may defeat proof of intent, and therefore, no crime can be proven.

270. A vice officer with information from a reliable informant goes to a certain vacant store building at night to investigate gambling. He listens at the back door of the building which is directly on an alley. He hears a clicking sound and voices making such statements as, "four is your point," "crapped out," and "coming out for ten." Through a small crack he observes a group of men gathered around a pool table, and observes money on the table. Someone apparently hears the officer, and when the men leave the table, the officer breaks down the barred door. Upon entry, he finds the men lounging around the room. No dice or other gambling equipment can be found.

Gambling with dice is a misdemeanor in most states, and the officer must actually witness the playing before an arrest can be made. Some city and county ordinances prohibit persons being in a place that is barricaded, in which case all persons present therein may be arrested. The fact that the gambling equipment cannot be found should not deter the officer from taking police action. Assistance should be requested from other officers to make a thorough search of the premises and parties.

271. A vice officer observes a known bookmaker engage in short conversations with numerous people, accept money from them, write something on the palm of his hand with an indelible pencil, then go to a public telephone and make a call after each conversation.

Bookmaking is a felony in most states, for which the person may be arrested upon reasonable or probable cause. In addition, to arresting for a state law violation, some cities and counties have ordinances which prohibit the possession of betting markers.

272. A vice officer attempting to gain entry to make a gambling arrest kicks in the wrong apartment door.

The officer should attempt to make the gambling arrest by locating the correct room, after which the owner or tenant of the room could be contacted and the circumstances regarding the mistake could be explained. In this situation, the office of the city attorney should be contacted for advice. Written reports should be made. Some departments require that photographs be taken in all situations where the city might incur a liability.

273. A vice squad officer observes a man and a woman get out of a taxi, go into a hotel with no luggage, and register. They go to an assigned room, and the officer observes them engage in sexual intercourse. The officer identifies himself, gains admittance, and arrests the couple for violating a municipal ordinance or resorting for fornication. The couple claim that they are married.

A claim of marriage is not proof of marriage, hence the officer should separate the parties and question them minutely regarding a time, place of ceremony, and parties present. If the stories coincide, the officer should give the parties the benefit of the doubt and leave after apologizing. In this latter situation, a written report should be made noting the time and any witnesses and their statements should be incorporated therein. If the officer is convinced that no marriage took place, an arrest may be made under the appropriate city or county ordinance prohibiting such action.

However, in some states, such as California, sexual intercourse between unmarried persons is *not* a crime. Hence no arrests could be made under these circumstances.

274. A vice officer receives a complaint from a known prostitute with a criminal record that her common law husband beats her and makes her work as a prostitute and makes her give him all of the money she earns.

Local laws will govern the situation in the various states. A crime report should be taken from the woman. It may be possible to arrest the man for violation of the laws pertaining to pimping or pandering. Pimping, a felony, can be described as: "Soliciting for, receiving compensation for soliciting, or deriving support from the money received by a prostitute."

Pandering could be described as: "Procuring a female to become an inmate in a house of prostitution or in any place in which prostitution is allowed or encouraged," and is generally a felony.

275. A vice officer receives a complaint from a citizen about an "after hours" bar which is frequented by "influential" persons.

Departmental policy will dictate which procedures should be utilized in the situation. However, the general method of operation would be to send an undercover operator into the bar to verify the complaint. If a violation of the liquor act is present, the officer should proceed as usual, which means that, using marked money, a buy is made, noting the time of the offense, and seizing the drink, arresting the server, securing money from the person or cash register, and booking the offender. If the officer is apprehensive about repercussions, it would be advisable to take a photographer along to photograph the premises and all therein. The mere presence of other persons in a bar after closing hours is not a violation of any law in most states, but it is usually a violation for a person to serve a consumer liquor in an on-sale establishment between specified hours.

276. A narcotics officer, standing outside a door, hears the persons inside the room state:
"Hey man, I need a fix. Do you have one?"
"Yeah."
Then the officer hears water running.

These facts indicate that there is reasonable or probable cause to believe that a felony is being committed. Two possible courses of action seem appropriate in this situation. First, the officer could kick in the door (not necessary to make an announcement where evidence may be destroyed) and make an arrest and a search. The second course would be to set up a stakeout in order to determine if this room is being used by several addicts or peddlers. Sometimes an immediate arrest might not be the best action, especially if there is a possibility of learning of a larger commercial traffic in narcotics.

277. A man stops the beat officer and demands that he get back the $500 he just spent in a low class bar which employs "hostesses."

There is no law against stupidity, per se. There must be a crime involved before the officer is justified in seizing any money, and then the money must be capable of being identified. The general procedure would be to refer the victim to the vice officer, who may be able to return to the bar with the victim and settle the matter amicably. The vice officer may follow up to ascertain if any laws are being violated by the bar.

278. An officer on patrol observes a group of persons circled at the rear of a vacant lot. Upon investigation, he finds a cock fight in progress.

Being present at a place where birds or animals may be engaged in an exhibition of fighting is a misdemeanor, and the officer should proceed to secure assistance, and then make as many arrests as possible, seizing the animals as evidence.

279. A citizen is about to be arrested by vice officers for "resorting for sexual intercourse," a misdemeanor under an ordinance. He displays credentials as a licensed private investigator, and claims he "bought the service" for the purpose of promoting good will and gaining information on a case under investigation.

Usually, the law prohibiting "resorting for the purpose of sexual intercourse" does not provide that the person have a reason for engaging in sexual intercourse. Hence it would seem that the reason why this person is participating in this crime is immaterial. The vice officers could proceed to book as they would any other ordinary "resorting" case. Departmental policy will dictate as to whether or not the male person is released or booked. Some departments make it a policy of only booking the prostitute and taking the name and address of the male subject, who is then released. Other departments follow the policy of booking both participants to the crime and letting the court make its dispositions as to the penalty for each of the parties.

280. A prostitute desires to file a complaint or report of rape.

From a legal standpoint, it is possible for a prostitute to be a victim of the crime of rape. If the interviewing officer is convinced that the complaint is valid, a written crime report should be made by the officer and signed by the victim. Generally, it is advisable to take the victim to a hospital for examination by a doctor for evidence of rape and treatment for any injuries.

If the injuries are pertinent to the case, photographs should be taken. The photographer should have another female present (policewoman, stenographer, or filing clerk) when photographing the victim's private areas. Any evidence collected should be preserved and booked, or filed, according to departmental procedure.

281. How can uniformed officers suppress wide-open gambling activities at late hours, when no vice squad men are available.

One of the most effective ways to suppress gambling is to make arrests. It is suggested that uniformed officers confer with their supervisor regarding the possibility of changing clothes into those which fit the area concerned, so that they may unobstrusively mingle with the participants, watching who is participating therein, and make some on the spot arrests. If departmental

regulations permit the use of informers, it may be possible to enlist the services of some friends of the department to assist in the operation.

**282. A man is approached by a prostitute to join her in an act of sexual
intercourse for which she will receive $20.00. As they leave the motel,
after completion of the act, the man refuses to pay. The prostitute says
she will report the incident to the police immediately. The man relates
the story to the police.**

The man should be referred to the vice officer. The vice officer should take
all the information available so that the prostitute could be "operated" and
an arrest made. It may be possible to use the man as a prosecuting witness,
although this rarely occurs. It would also be rare for the prostitute to make
a complaint. If it was possible to prosecute a person upon his mere conversation alone, then complaints may be sought against each, but such is
not usually done.

**283. An officer newly assigned to vice duties has difficulty in making ar-
rests of prostitutes.**

Officers working plain clothes or vice could:
    1. Act like a potential customer.
    2. Obtain name and address of a former customer and get him to intro-
duce you.
    3. Use another prostitute to introduce you.
    4. Use a bartender, taxi driver, or other sources to get an introduction.
    5. If you have a partner, say in a loud voice where you can be overheard
by the prostitute, "I'd give fifty dollars for a good time."
    The officer must always be careful not to develop a case by entrapment.

**284. A uniformed patrol officer obtains information indicating the exis-
tence of a vice condition.**

The general rule is that an officer should proceed to make an arrest when
the facts legally justify an arrest. If the facts are insufficient to merit an immediate physical arrest, the officer should make a complete written report
of the suspected vice condition for a follow-up investigation by a plainclothes officer.

In the event action seems imperative, and a uniformed officer would
"burn up" the suspected location, he may request his superior officer to
dispatch an investigator to meet him out of sight of the place or situation
to be investigated. In some instances the uniformed officer could change to
plain clothes and follow through with his investigations.

All officers should be mindful that a suspect may be an officer assigned
to vice investigation, therefore if it is discovered that a "suspect" is a vice
investigator, the case should be concluded without disclosing to anyone that
the officer was recognized. Instead, it is a good police technique to book

the "suspect" (officer) as though he were one of the offenders. After the booking has been completed he may be "bailed out" by a "friend." This keeps the vice investigator's real identity from being revealed.

285. A mother complains that her minor son was served liquor at the corner bar.

Serving liquor to a minor is a misdemeanor in most states. These complaints are best handled by the vice officer who may then "operate" the bar for these and other violations that may have occurred. A complete report of the complaint should be made.

286. A man explains that he was involved in an illegal poker game and was cheated out of $2,000.00 by two other players in the same game, and that he can prove how he was cheated.

Participating in an illegal poker game is a misdemeanor. However, mere participation in a crime of this nature will not keep a participant from being a victim, hence a crime report should be taken from him for theft (bunco). Generally, this type of investigation is handled best by the vice officer or detectives assigned to handle bunco investigations.

287. An officer directing traffic is confronted by a person who points out a woman and complains that on the previous night someone stole his pants while he was having intercourse with her in a cheap hotel nearby.

Entering a room with intent to steal sometimes constitutes burglary—a felony. If the victim wishes to make a crime report for said crime, it would seem that an arrest of the woman for burglary would be in order. This is not unusual as an occurrence, but it is unusual for the victim to complain in such a situation. Whatever action is taken, the vice officer should be alerted as to the incident so that some attention may be given to the person involved and the hotel. Proper investigation may disclose the use of an accomplice by the woman, which may lead to a prosecution for conspiracy to steal or commit burglary.

SEX OFFENSES

288. In a secluded spot an officer encounters a man and a woman embraced in sexual intercourse; each is married to another person. The woman is very cooperative towards the officer's questioning. However, the man refuses to answer any questions or produce any identification and is very antagonistic.

Sexual intercouse, per se, is no crime. The fact that each is married to some other person may constitute grounds for divorce in some states, but that is a mere civil matter, with which the officer should not be concerned. The attitude of the man indicates that he should be taken to the station where a more minute inquiry may be made as to his identity, and his refusal to produce any identification. Sometimes it is necessary to take the finger-prints of such a person and check them before releasing the person from custody. If, however, the act is committed in view of others, it would consti-tute offensive conduct under disturbing the peace, a misdemeanor.

289. An individual appears nightly in a bar on an officer's beat dressed in female clothing, but displays such masculine features as beard shadow, low-pitched voice, and generally gives indications of being a sex deviate.

There is no law prohibiting a person from being a sex deviate, or queer. Perverts may roam at large providing they do not practice certain prohibited acts. One such prohibited act is usually found in city and county ordinances to the effect that no one shall masquerade in the garb of the opposite sex. If such ordinance prevails in your jurisdiction, it would seem appropriate to take the person into custody and book him for masquerading. It is also suggested that a full length photograph be taken of the subject while he is dressed in woman's clothing, to be used as evidence in court, if that be-comes necessary. A clear violation should be established before a booking is made.

290. A woman complains that she is spied upon while taking nude sun-baths, by a man with binoculars on the roof of an apartment building a few doors up the street.

It may be suggested to the woman that perhaps she is in violation of the laws relating to indecent exposure. The use of binoculars in this situation would not seem to stamp the man as being a Peeping Tom. Peeping Tom cases are usually relegated to those wherein the person is trespassing personally upon private property and peeking into a door or window of a house. In such a case, the Peeping Tom is in violation of disturbing the peace, a misdemeanor.

In addition to suggesting that the woman may be in violation of the law, the officer could also suggest that a bikini would be appropriate.

291. In answering a disturbance of the peace call an officer is met by an elderly man who complains that two boys, 8 and 10 years of age, threw rocks at him. The boys admit this but state they did so because the man had exposed himself to them.

Officers must exercise their own good judgment in concluding who is telling the truth in this situation. Throwing rocks at another person may constitute a simple assault. On the other hand, a person who exposes himself is com-mitting a misdemeanor of indecent exposure under most state laws, and in some states, this act may constitute a felony. It is also possible in this situation for the boys, age 8 and 10, to make a citizen's or "private person" arrest. It may be advisable to secure the assistance of a juvenile officer who may be more experienced in questioning juveniles.

292. Patrol officers check a parked car in a secluded area with two persons in the front seat who are necking. Both persons are adult males.

Between two normal male persons this would constitute an unusual action, but between two perverts or homosexuals this would be normal. There is no law against homosexuals per se, but only against their unusual practices. Once such practice is the offensive conduct of two males kissing, which would constitute a misdemeanor under most state laws. Departmental policy will dictate whether to make appropriate field interrogation cards and release or to make an arrest.

293. An officer observes a male person approach servicemen, talk for a few moments, and then hasten away. The servicemen state that the person solicited them to participate in an homosexual act.

This act is a misdemeanor, for which a person should be arrested either by the officer who overhears the conversation or by the persons solicited. Another technique would be to keep this obvious pervert under observation and follow him until some crime is committed in the presence of the officer. In any event, the pervert should be stopped, a field investigation card should be made, and a "make" or want should be run on him before he is released or arrested. There is no law against being a homosexual, but laws do prohibit practicing homosexual acts.

294. A citizen reports to police that two male persons are living next door as man and wife.

In most states, when two persons of the opposite sex live together, no crime is committed. When two male persons live together as man and wife, some question arises as to the laws pertaining to perverts and masquerading. This type of complaint should be given to the vice officer for follow-up investigation. The vice officer could check for violations of laws pertaining to perverts and masquerading.

295. On the person of a misdemeanor offender, a police officer finds an extortion letter.

The mere possession of an extortion letter is no offense. These facts, however, should prompt the officer to conduct a thorough investigation as to extortion complaints. These matters should usually be handled by the bunco officer or detectives assigned to handle extortion and blackmail matters. A check should be made for an accomplice being in on the proposed extortion, because it could possibly amount to a conspiracy to commit extortion.

296. An officer receives a call from a woman who states that she has received a very indecent phone call.

This type of action constitutes a misdemeanor. The officer should first obtain all of the facts regarding the exact words used, and determine if this call is one of a series of a like nature, if the victim is aware of the identity of the caller, and whether she wishes to prosecute. If the victim does not desire to prosecute, advise her to have her phone number changed by the telephone company to an unlisted number. If prosecution is desired, the officer should instruct the victim to make a date with the suspect the next time he calls. The victim should be instructed that after the suspect calls that she should not telephone the police department immediately, but should wait approximately one half hour before making any calls, because a clever suspect may phone back to see whether or not the victim is making calls out. If it is ascertained that the suspect does not know the victim, a policewoman may be substituted for her to keep the date. If the victim is to meet the suspect, it should not be at his apartment, but should be at the victim's place or in some public place. The victim should be instructed to ask the suspect at the meeting to repeat his conversation over the phone in order to establish positive identification, after which she may drop a handkerchief or make some other prearranged signal so that the officer staked out may close in for the arrest. If no policewoman is used, this would be a misdemeanor not committed in the presence of the officers and the victim would thereupon make the arrest.

297. A 13-year-old girl complains to an officer that a man had exposed himself to her about 15 or 20 minutes before. The officer apprehends the described suspect about half an hour later and takes him to the station where the girl establishes positive identification.

Generally, such an act constitutes a misdemeanor which must be committed in the presence of an officer before he can make an arrest. But the victim may make a citizen's arrest. The usual crime and arrest reports should be signed by the victim and the offender should be booked to the victim as the arresting person. Another procedure would call for taking a report of all the facts from the victim, releasing the suspect, and obtaining a warrant from the court the next day. This action is preferred when there is some doubt as to the veracity of the girl's story. A policewoman or matron make good interrogators in such situations.

298. While on patrol in a residential district at about 11:00 p.m., officers observe a well-dressed man run across an alley and into a backyard. A few seconds later, this same man appears on the sidewalk in front of the property where he was first observed. He was stopped and asked to identify himself. The man refuses to answer any of the questions put to him by the officers and states, "I'm an honest citizen, and you police can't question me like this." What should the officers do?

The problem involves the right of an officer to make a field interrogation. The answer contained in a leading appellate decision, "Gisske vs. Sanders,"

9 Cal. App. 13, 1908, states: "A police officer has a right to make inquiry in a proper manner of anyone upon the public streets at a late hour as to his identity and the occasion of his presence, if the surroundings are such as to indicate to a reasonable man that the public safety demands such identification. The fact that a crime or crimes had recently been committed in that neighborhood; that plaintiff at a late hour was found in the locality; that he refused to answer proper questions establishing his identity, were circumstances which should lead a reasonable officer to require his presence at the station, where the sergeant in charge might make more minute and careful inquiry."

299. A person complains that a neighbor across the street deliberately lighted some newspaper and threw it on the front seat of his car, burning the cushion. He put out the fire and called the officer. The neighbor is now across the street watering his lawn.

Such an action would constitute a felony and the person should be arrested in the usual manner after taking a crime report from the victim. This action is covered by state laws which read similar to the following: "Any person who willfully and maliciously sets fire to or burns or causes to be burned or who aids, counsels or procures the burning of any barrack, cock, crib, rick or stack of hay, corn, wheat, oats, barley, or other grain of any kind; or any pile of coal, wood or other fuel; or any street-car, railway car, ship, boat or other water craft, automobile or other motor vehicle; or any other personal property not herein specifically named; (such property being of the value of twenty-five dollars and the property of another person) shall upon conviction thereof, be sentenced to the penitentiary for not less than one or more than three years."

300. An officer receives an "attempt suicide" call, and upon arrival, the woman states that she had swallowed some sleeping pills but refuses to be taken to the hospital.

Since attempted suicide is no crime in some states, no arrest can usually be made. However, the officer should immediately call for an ambulance and if no ambulance is available, the officer should transport the attempted suicide victim in the police car to an emergency hospital. Although under most state laws this person is performing a legal act, one of the duties of an officer is to save lives and he should make every effort to do so, even to the extent of forcibly taking this person to the hospital. After the hospital has completed its treatment of the victim, the officer should make a complete written report of the incident. If there is some question regarding the sanity of the individual, see situation 328.

301. An officer patrolling the boardwalk at the beach is stopped by a woman who complains "that blond hussy in the white bikini suit should be arrested for indecent exposure."

Voluntary indecent exposure of one's own body constitutes a crime, usually a misdemeanor. The term "indecent exposure" refers to that which would be offensive or shock the sensibilities of an average person. Since some persons are more easily offended or shocked than others, the officer must project his thinking as to what he thinks a jury would consider sufficient for a conviction.

The officer should take the name and address of the complaining person. Perhaps the complainant could accompany the officer to the suspected offender. If police action is indicated, the officer may either make a physical arrest or have the complainant sign a complaint for the issuance of a warrant for arrest. It is further recommended that when an immediate arrest is made, that full length photographs be taken, for presentation as evidence in court.

302. An officer in answering a disturbance of the peace call meets a woman who complains that her landlord prowls her room in her absence.

Although a landlord is allowed reasonable rights of visitation to inspect the upkeep of his property, such visits must be made at reasonable times and should be made while the tenant is present. Some attempt should be made to get the landlord and the woman together and agree as to how and when such inspections are to be made. If the woman is still dissatisfied, advise her to put another lock on the door and advise her that she should make herself available so that the landlord may inspect the interior at reasonable times. Consistent unauthorized entries even by a landlord may constitute a misdemeanor.

303. A person is caught exposing himself in a public park and he identifies himself as a foreign consul, prominent citizen or governmental official.

If a person is a foreign consul, he may not be arrested for a misdemeanor because the United States has treaties with foreign countries giving such persons limited immunity. The arrest of the other persons may be handled as an ordinary citizen and if the action is witnessed by the officers, the persons could be arrested. Generally, such violations are misdemeanors unless children are present, then these persons may be arrested for a felony. Certainly it should never be contended that a person should be given any preferential treatment just because he is a prominent citizen or because of his status or situation in life.

304. A beat officer is confronted by a person who states that he had reported a $20 camera as having been stolen a week ago and he now sees his camera in the window of a pawn shop a few doors away.

The officer should accompany the owner back to the pawn shop and ask the person in charge of the pawn shop to produce the camera for inspection. If it is identified as his camera, the negotiations should then be between the owner and the pawn shop person. The officer should have no part in assisting in negotiation for the return of the property other than to preserve the peace. If negotiations are unsuccessful between the parties concerned, the officer should call the detective detail assigned to pawn shop investigations. Generally speaking, the pawn shops are under the control of the police departments and cooperate in returning property to the rightful owner. If such cooperation is not forthcoming, the officer should proceed to institute inquiry as to whether or not this pawn shop should stay in business.

305. An officer receives a call, "man down." Upon arrival, the officer sees a man lying on the sidewalk kicking his feet. The man soon recovers and tells the officer that he is an epileptic but does not wish medical treatment.

A person who is able to take care of himself may refuse to receive medical treatment. If the officer feels that the patient is able to carry on or take care of himself without assistance, then compliance with the wishes of the epileptic would seem proper. A written report of the incident should be made and a copy of same forwarded to the State Motor Vehicle Department. Most state laws prohibit an epileptic from driving a motor vehicle.

306. Officers are given witness subpoenas to serve. One is for a doctor. As the officers arrive at the doctor's office and talk to the nurse, the doctor is seen to enter his office. The nurse uses the intercom to inform the doctor why the officers are there and the doctor states that he refuses to be served.

Most state laws governing the service of a subpoena provide: "A subpoena may be served by any person, but a peace officer must serve in his county any subpoena delivered to him for service, either on the part of the people or of the defendant, and must, without delay, make a written return of the service, subscribed by him, stating the time and place of service. The service is made by showing the original to the witness personally and informing him of its contents." Under the section here presented, and with the situation here existing, a stakeout would seem to be in order because there is generally no requirement that a person must accept service of a subpoena unless it is made in the prescribed manner as above mentioned.

307. An officer answers a call to a restaurant where the manager points out a customer who refuses to pay for his dinner. The customer states the food was no good, although he ate it.

Officers should follow the usual procedure in situations like this by asking the party the reason for his actions. It may be that there was something wrong with the food or that the person has no money. Officers are not charged with the duty of collecting for persons. However, it should be explained to both parties that there are laws which may be applicable to this situation. One state's law provides: "Any person who obtains any food or accommodations at a hotel, restaurant, boarding-house, lodging-house, furnished apartment house, furnished bungalow court, or furnished auto camp, without paying therefor, with intent to defraud the proprietor or manager thereof, or who obtains credit at a hotel, inn, restaurant, boarding-house, lodging-house, furnished apartment house, furnished bungalow courts, or furnished auto camp, by the use of any false pretense, or who, after obtaining credit, food, accommodations, at a hotel, inn, restaurant, boarding-house, lodging-house, or furnished apartment house, furnished bungalow court, or furnished auto camp, absconds, or surreptitiously, or by force, menace, or threats, removes any part of his baggage therefrom, without paying for his food or accommodations is guilty of a misdemeanor." If such a law exists, an arrest may be justified, but if there is no intent to defraud, it would be a civil matter only.

308. A person complains to officers that a one-legged man is begging on the sidewalk in violation of a local ordinance.

This activity is covered by some state laws or local ordinances which provide: "Every beggar who solicits alms as a business is a vagrant," a misdemeanor. If an arrest seems necessary, the name of the complaining witness should be obtained and incorporated in the arrest report. It may also be deemed advisable to obtain a signed crime report from the complaining witness before an arrest is made. In this situation, a private person has as much right as an officer to make an arrest. The situation may be such that a warning to the beggar will remedy the violation.

JUVENILE

309. A mother complains that her sixteen-year-old daughter stays out late at night and she wants the police to make her stay at home.

Probably the first approach to this problem would be to advise the mother to bring her daughter to the juvenile unit for counselling by a policewoman. Pending such action, the officer could advise the mother and the daughter regarding the violation of the curfew law which most cities have and are worded as follows: "Every person under the age of eighteen years who loiters about the public streets, avenues, alleys, parks, or public places between the hours of ten o'clock p.m. and the time of sunrise of the following day when not accompanied by his parent or legal guardian having legal custody and control of such person, or spouse of such person over twenty-one years of age, is guilty of a misdemeanor. Every parent, guardian, or other person having the legal care, custody, or control of any person under the age of eighteen years who allows or permits such person to violate any provision of this ordinance is guilty of a misdemeanor. Violation of this ordinance or any provision thereof is punishable by a fine not exceeding five hundred dollars ($500.00) or by imprisonment in the city jail of said city or in the county jail, at the discretion of the committing magistrate, for a period not exceeding six months, or by both fine and imprisonment." The mother could also be advised to seek help from her church or from a community social service agency.

310. An officer is called upon to conduct an investigation of a student regarding a theft. The student is in class at school.

An officer desiring to question or arrest a student on school grounds or during school hours should first contact the school principal or vice-principal and explain the reason for seeing the student. At the same time a request for permission to use an office or room for questioning or permission to take the student from the school for interviewing should be made. If the student is to be placed under arrest, this should be explained to the officials of the school as a matter of good public relations. It would not seem advisable to enter a classroom in session in order to make an arrest. This type of police courtesy would also apply to churches and club meetings where an arrest might disrupt the proceedings and possibly create a feeling of ill will.

311. Juvenile officers acting on complaints of neighbors investigate a home where they find a twenty-year-old baby sitter (not a relative) in a drunken condition, and two small infants in filthy surroundings, no food in the house, and in an obviously undernourished condition. The widowed mother is away working.

The officers should:
1. Take photographs of the condition of the premises.
2. Record statements made by the complaining neighbors.
3. Book the drunk under the appropriate city or county ordinance.
4. Take the infants to the detention home.
5. Lock the premises and leave a note as to what was done with the infants.
6. Contact the mother regarding making other arrangements for the care of the children and call her attention to the possibility that she may be violating a state law pertaining to the care of children.

312. An officer receives a complaint from the principal of an elementary school that a man has been loitering about the school for about two hours. Upon questioning the suspect, the man tells the officer that he has a son enrolled in the school and that he was merely investigating the school premises to see what the conditions were.

The officer should check the story of the suspect, and if true, such facts should be conveyed to the principal of the school. If it is found that the man is not telling the truth, he should be taken to the station and checked out for crime reports or teletypes as being a possible felony suspect for molesting children. If the person's description fits, he should be arrested for that particular crime. In any event, the person could be arrested for loitering about school premises without lawful business, usually prohibited by state law.

313. An adult is seen stopping his flower-laden truck at busy intersections and putting several pails of flowers and a juvenile on the sidewalk to make sales.

The officer should check the adult for a city license to peddle. Also the juvenile should be checked for a work permit. Generally, the juvenile should not be taken into custody, but a complete report should be filed listing names, addresses, time, place, and possible violations, and copies forwarded to the juvenile officer.

314. A neighbor complains that two children, a boy of fourteen and a girl of twelve, have been left at home for a week. Their parents went east because of a death in the family.

It is usually appropriate to have the juvenile officer handle such cases. The juvenile officer could check the children regarding proper care, food, school attendance, etc. There is possible prosecution of the parents in this situation for lack of supervision. Departmental policies will dictate actions of the juvenile officer.

315. An officer on patrol picks up a boy who claims that he was forced to have sexual intercourse with several girls in a car parked off the highway. The car is still there, but the girls have gone.

This story seems incredible, but it is an actual case. The procedure followed was to check the car for ownership, contact the registered owner, and take the boy to the station for further interrogation. The car, of course, was examined for possible evidence in support of the boy's story, and the car was impounded. The girls were arrested at their homes and taken to the station where they were interrogated by the juvenile officers. They were referred to the juvenile court and found delinquent. The wording of the state statute precluded a finding of rape against the girls.

316. The mother of a 13-year-old girl complains that her child has been raped by a neighbor boy 13 years old.

Juvenile officers should be called to assist in this case. Such happenings are not uncommon, but generally speaking, the victim should be taken immediately to the receiving hospital for examination and possible medical attention, after which the boy and his parents could be brought to the station for proper investigation. Complete reports should be made of what was disclosed and appropriate action taken.

317. A citizen complains that children have been playing with matches in her front hedge and that one fire already has started as a result of it.

It would seem appropriate for the officer to locate the parents of the children and have the parents take remedial action with their own children, rather than have the officer handle the situation. The latter action, of course, is recommended if the parents cannot be located. It would also seem advisable to make a written report regarding the complaint of the citizen.

318. A woman approaches the beat officer at a busy downtown intersection and states that her little boy is lost.

The beat officer should take a complete description of the lost boy and radio or telephone into headquarters regarding the situation. Headquarters could then alert other cars and beat officers regarding the description of the boy. Juvenile officers should be contacted because they are usually experinced in locating lost children. They know, for example, that lost children often migrate to candy stores, toy departments in department stores, theaters, restrooms, etc. The mother should be advised to assist in the search and if the child is not immediately located, a formal missing persons report should be filed.

319. An officer is conducting an interrogation of a juvenile suspect at headquarters. The irate father arrives, assumes an extremely protective attitude, is belligerent to the officer, and demands immediate unconditional release of his son.

The officer should always realize that parents become emotional and are not entirely reasonable when their children are involved in some difficulty. This means that an unusual amount of tolerance should be expected from the officer when dealing with irate parents. Patience and tact should govern the actions of the officer and he should not arrest the father unless some crime is committed against the officer, such as battery. In event of the latter, the father should be arrested. The juvenile should be detained until the interrogation is complete, and the disposition of the juvenile has been decided. The father should be informed of the facts of the case and what action the officer expects to take regarding the child.

320. An officer apprehends a juvenile pulling a fire alarm box. During response of the fire apparatus one has an accident, and a fireman is killed.

Such an offense is a felony, and the juvenile should be taken into custody, and processed according to departmental policy. A complete investigation should be made of the incident, and appropriate reports filed.

321. On a routine patrol, an officer comes upon a group of juveniles on a vacant lot. They have a case of beer, some of it open, in their possession.

The juveniles should be apprehended and taken to the station, along with the case of beer. Generally, the procedure is to call the parents of the juveniles and release the juveniles to the parents. Sometimes juveniles are arrested and booked for being delinquent and then released. The beer should be booked as evidence and the open bottles should be sealed before being booked. The juvenile officer may follow up on the case, and should make the final police disposition.

322. An officer is called when a small child is found alone and crying in a locked car.

This is a misdemeanor under most state laws, which generally read:
"No person shall leave standing a locked vehicle in which there is any person who cannot readily escape therefrom."
The officer should:
1. Search for parents, and explain the law to them.
2. Make a complaint and secure a warrant if the situation so demands.
3. Break open the car and take the child to the detention home or appropriate facility.
4. Make the appropriate written reports.

323. A crowd of juveniles congregate at a certain location, to the annoyance of nearby residents.

The officer could:
1. Contact residents and others and assure them of your interest in their problem.
2. Cite the owner of the premises to the office of the prosecuting attorney for an office hearing.
3. Notify the owner of the possibility of filing suit for abatement of a nuisance.
4. Suggest to the owner that he hire a special officer to eject the trouble makers.
5. Obtain all necessary identification from the juveniles and note the times of occurrence. They could be advised to disperse and if they refuse to do so, they could be placed under arrest for disturbing the peace.

324. A citizen informs police that several minors are defacing the walls of a public restroom.

If department regulations do not call for booking of minors, they should at least be taken to the station and turned over to juvenile officers for processing. Written reports should always be made in such situations as to the acts and facts surrounding the incident. Sometimes, it may be desirable to photograph the defaced wall as evidence.

If departmental regulations allow booking of minors, the officer could arrest the minors for malicious mischief, if observation verifies the defacement.

325. Police are informed by a juvenile that a gang fight is planned.

This information is of particular importance to the officer working in the juvenile detail or to officers who may be assigned to gang details. The watch commander should be alerted so that more patrol cars could be seen in that particular area prior to the time the fight is to commence. It is considered to be more important in these cases to prevent a fight than it is to wait until the fight develops and then arrest only those who can be caught.

MENTAL CASES

326. Officers answer a disturbance of the peace mental case call and find a 19-year-old mental case cutting up furniture with a knife in his mother's home. It takes six men to subdue him, after which the mother refuses to permit the officers to take him from the house. Neighbors state that this has happened before.

See Question 328 for a complete statement on the law on this subject. Under the facts of this case it would seem that the officers would be justified in forcibly restraining this person (preferably with restraining straps) and take him into the psychopathic ward of the hospital.

327. An officer answers a "mental case" call. The mental case is holding a loaded shotgun at his head and demands that the officer drive him several miles to his psychiatrist.

It would be the understatement of the year to say that mental cases are problems and should be approached with caution. Generally, this situation would call for three things:

    1. Distraction (engage the person in conversation or change the subject matter), then

    2. Disarm, and

    3. Arrest as a psychopath. (See situation 328.)

328. An officer answers a "female mental case" call and upon arrival meets a woman who complains that "people are shooting rays at me through the wall."

In this situation, the officer should first attempt to locate her husband, relatives, or friends to take care of her. Neighbors or witnesses may be able to furnish this information. In any event, the officer cannot make an arrest because a person is believed to be psychopathic. The law provides that the person must be so mentally disturbed as to be likely to cause injury to himself or others before an arrest can be made. This situation is covered in some state laws as follows: "When any person becomes so mentally ill as to be likely to cause injury to himself or others and to require immediate care, treatment, or restraint, a peace officer or health officer, who has reasonable cause to believe that such is the case, may take the person into custody and for his best interest and protection place him in custody as provided in this section. The person believed to be mentally ill may be admitted and detained in the quarters provided in any county hospital or state hospital upon application of the peace officer or health officer. The application shall be in writing and shall state the circumstances under which the person's condition was called to the officer's attention and shall also state that the officer believes, as a result of his personal observation, that the person is mentally ill and because of his illness is likely to injure himself or others if not immediately hospitalized. The superintendent or physician in charge of the quarters provided in such county hospital or state hospital may care for and treat the person for a period not to exceed seventy-two (72) hours. Within said seventy-two (72) hours, the person shall be discharged from the institution unless a petition of mental illness is presented to a judge of the superior court and the court issues an order for the detention of such person, or unless the person is admitted as a patient under any other provision of law."

329. An officer receives a disturbance call and upon arrival finds a citizen in his front yard holding his two-year-old son in his left arm and a butcher knife in his right hand. He threatens the child with the knife if the officer attempts to arrest him.

The officer should:

1. Not attempt an arrest.

2. Talk with the father until he is off-guard then seize him; but do not risk injury to the child.

3. Arrest as a psychopath. (See Question 328.)

4. Release the child to mother or other responsible person. If neither are available deliver the child to a detention home.

5. Make a written report.

CIVIL PROBLEMS

330. An officer answers a "see the man" call and finds a taxicab driver and his customer arguing about the charges.

The officers should attempt to ascertain who called the police. If it was a third party whose peace was being disturbed, it would probably be sufficient to warn the taxicab driver and his fare and to have them cease their activities. If they continue to argue and disturb someone, the name of that person can be included in the arrest report as a complaining witness for a violation of disturbing the peace, a misdemeanor.

Some cities have "evading taxicab payment of fare" ordinances in which case the taxicab driver could make an arrest for violation of the concerned ordinance.

331. An officer answers "a grand theft auto suspect being held by citizen" call and finds the suspect being held at the point of a gun by the citizen. The suspect is a repossessor who was removing the car from the citizen's driveway.

The officer should advise both parties that repossession is a civil matter and that the police do not have jurisdiction. As to the pointing of the gun, a person has a legal right to protect his property if it is his. As to repossession of the car it may be taken only in accordance with terms of the contract and civil law governing repossessions. (See Appendix E.)

If any laws have been violated in the presence of the officers an arrest may be made.

332. An officer answers an "unknown trouble" call and finds a woman who wants her common law husband to move out. The man states that he has been living with her for several years, but is not married to her, and he won't move out because he pays the bills and owns the furniture.

This is a civil matter, and as far as the facts are stated there is no cause for the officer to take action other than to keep the peace. This means that if the woman wishes to move out, the "husband" could not prevent her from moving. The converse is also true, so that if the "husband" wishes to move out the woman could not prevent him from so doing. If any disturbance is caused in the presence of the officer which annoys any of the neighbors, then there is a possibility that an arrest could be made for disturbing the peace. The parties should be advised to settle their differences in a friendly manner or to see an attorney. Even though there are no common law marriages in many states, the officer should not attempt to determine the civil rights of the individual parties.

333. An officer on patrol is stopped by a citizen who complains that a mechanic has done more work to his vehicle than was authorized, and the mechanic will not release the vehicle until the full amount is paid.

This is generally a civil matter, and usually comes under the heading of a "mechanic's lien." This means that the mechanic is entitled to retain possession of a vehicle upon which he has made repairs or performed labor until an arrangement for payment of the bill has been made. Sometimes a mechanic's lien is only applicable up to $100 and all charges in excess of that amount are not subject to the lien unless the legal owner has authorized work in excess of that amount. The officer should merely preserve the peace and make a written report of the incident.

334. A woman apartment house manager complains to an officer on patrol that her husband rented an apartment without her authority. The woman wants the officer to remove the illegal occupants.

The officer should advise the woman that this is purely a civil matter, and that she should consult with an attorney. A record should be made of the advice given by the officer.

335. A landlord complains to an officer that one of his tenants is cooking in his room, and that this is against "house rules."

A landlord can make reasonable rules regarding his premises. However, these rules are not penal in character, and therefore the officer should advise the landlord that they cannot take any legal action. Instead, the landlord should be told that he should proceed by civil process in securing an eviction, if necessary. In this connection, it should be suggested that the landlord secure the services of an attorney for appropriate legal civil action.

336. The owner of a vehicle complains to the patrol officer that a painter on an overhead scaffold splattered paint on his car which was legally parked at the curb.

The officer should immediately interview the painter to ascertain whether the act was accidental or on purpose. If the act was intentional the painter may be arrested (or a warrant may be secured for his arrest) for maliciously injuring the property of another. In the event that the act would seem to be accidental, the motorist should be advised that it is a civil matter and that he should consult his attorney or insurance company. It would also be appropriate to ascertain if the painter is licensed or has a permit to do business in the city or county concerned. Under no circumstances should the officer attempt to act as a "collection agency" for the injured party.

337. A local merchant reports that a man gave him a check on Saturday and said to hold it until Monday afternoon, and that he would make a deposit Monday morning. Tuesday, the check came back "No Account."

In all types of issuing checks, there must be an intent to defraud before criminal action can be taken. When a person gives another person a check with the promise to hold it, this amounts to a promissory note, the collection of which must proceed by civil action. Under the facts of the situation, this check is a mere promissory note, and the person should be informed that it is a civil matter.

338. An agent for a finance company asks you to go with him to repossess a car.

Since this is a civil matter, the officer should not participate in repossession of a car. The general rules on repossession are covered in Appendix E.

INVESTIGATIONS

339. An officer asks: "Since the patrol force is the backbone of the police department, and conducts preliminary investigations, how far should these preliminary investigations be carried?"

In conducting investigations by the patrol officers, it would be dependent upon the size of the department and its unit responsibilities. For a small department with a small investigation division the patrol officer would conduct an investigation as far as possible. This would mean from answering the complaint, interviewing informants and witnesses, if any, to investigation of the crime scene, taking photographs, preserving evidence, dusting for fingerprints, and interrogation of suspects. Conducting this type of an investigation would at times be of some advantage to the investigators when they take over the case, as they would have the information to work with. However, in a large department the patrol officers would arrive at the crime scene and interview the informant and any witnesses and protect the crime scene for the preservation of evidence until the investigators arrived along with technicians from the crime laboratory. A general rule would be to permit the patrol officers to pursue the preliminary investigation if within their tour of duty or, if within a reasonable amount of overtime it may be completed and if the officers would not be away from patrol duties an unreasonable length of time or, if the investigation does not involve other jurisdictions.

340. At the scene of a crime the first officer to arrive conducts a brief interview with the victim or witnesses, then puts out a radio broadcast concerning the missing suspect, but there is some uncertainty regarding the minimum amount of information to be broadcast.

Generally, the first officer on the scene obtains the information and makes the initial broadcast without unnecessary delay. It should include:
   Type of crime committed
   Type of premises attacked
   Location of occurrence
   Number, sex, and race (or ethnic group) of suspect(s)
   Any unusual descriptions of suspect(s)
   Direction taken from scene
   Mode of travel—on foot or auto
   Describe auto, if used
   Weapon(s) used
   After the initial broadcast has been made, more information may be obtained and a more complete broadcast sent. The primary objective is to alert other police units near the area concerned to be on the lookout for the suspects.

341. Protection of crime scene by an officer.

The purpose of protecting the crime scene is to prevent the removal, destruction, rearrangement, or concealment of evidence. The patrolman, normally the first to arrive at the crime scene, takes necessary steps for the protection of life and property; arrests the perpetrator or detains the suspect; and removes all persons from the immediate vicinity of the crime in order to prevent possible destruction of evidence. If possible, he prohibits all persons who have knowledge of the crime from leaving the area and records their names and addresses; takes preliminary statements; denies access to all unauthorized persons not involved in the crime; and notes and records any fact pertinent to the crime.

342. Search for latent fingerprints at crime scene.

The key to discovery of fingerprints is proper reconstruction of the movements of the perpetrator and examination of each object that he may have touched. Particular attention is given to the places where the perpetrator may have made his entrance and exit. If the entrance or exit was made through a door, the investigator examines the knob, panels, and framework of the door for fingerprints; if through a window, he examines the panes, sashes, and framework of the window. The presence of latent fingerprints may be revealed by the use of cross-lighting or a large reading glass. An oblique beam from a flashlight aimed at different angles may disclose prints that would otherwise remain invisible. Breathing upon a surface may also disclose fingerprints.

343. Uniformed officers are first at the scene of a homicide. Newspaper reporters demand immediate permission to take photographs in order to make a deadline.

Officers may permit reporters to take photographs of the scene at a distance so as not to disturb the area of the crime scene. It would be keeping good press relations and would also be preserving evidence of the crime scene. This also may be of some help to the department in that the photographs taken by the reporters may reveal some type of evidence in their pictures that may possibly be missed by the investigators.

If the situation demands, the officers may tell the reporters not to approach the crime scene, that it is being guarded to preserve evidence. Any reporter that would approach, so as to interfere, should be informed by the officers that they may be in violation of a state law for interfering with a police investigation.

344. At the scene of a homicide, officers find a large amount of jewelry or money near the body but there is nothing to establish that the property belonged to the deceased who evidently had met death by violence. The coroner states that he will take custody of the property.

Generally speaking, a coroner could take custody of the property, but if this is done a signed receipt should be obtained from the person taking control of such property. As to other items, some departments pursue the following:

"*Suicide notes:* Original suicide notes shall accompany the body to a coroner's mortuary. Portions of suicide notes pertaining to the suicidal act shall be quoted in the death report when practicable. When a copy of the original suicide note is desired by investigating officers, a copy may be obtained from the coroner's office. When the original note is needed for crime laboratory study, it shall be obtained from the coroner's office by a member of the crime laboratory.

"*Poisons and drugs:* All poisons, drugs, and their containers suspected of being connected with a suicide shall accompany the body to the coroner's office.

"*Firearms:* A firearm suspected of being a suicide weapon may be booked as evidence for the purpose of ballistic tests. Concerned investigators shall release such weapon to the coroner's property office upon completion of the tests."

345. At the scene of a dead body, a deputy coroner desires to search the body for personal property.

Generally, the officer in charge at the scene of a dead body should prevent any person, other than an officer, from searching a body. In situations where the person was killed in an accident or during the commission of a crime, it may be necessary to search immediately for identification. In other situations, such as where a person dies at a home or apartment from apparently natural causes, it would probably be desirable to secure a witness or a relative of the deceased to be present when the body is searched for personal effects. In this latter case, it is sometimes the policy to permit the coroner to search the body, but a receipt should be obtained from him whenever personal effects and possessions of the deceased are taken by the coroner or his deputy. This receipt should be attached to the written report of the death.

346. An officer responds to a fire in which a person is found dead in the wreckage.

An officer first on the scene should secure the cooperation of the firemen to preserve the scene and admit no unauthorized persons therein. The officer should call the detectives for possible homicide investigation, after calling for an ambulance, because there is a possibility that the person may not be dead. Departmental regulations will dictate whether or not to call a photographer for pictures of the fire scene.

347. Officers are investigating a suspected burglary of a business establishment and the owner or manager insists on opening for the public before the investigation has been completed, and before the search for fingerprints is accomplished.

In such a situation the officers should protect the place of entry and take prints. Also, the area of the burglarous objective (cash register, safe, etc.) should be isolated until prints have been taken.

This situation indicated the desirability of training practically all field officers and investigators on how to look for and lift latent fingerprints. Portable fingerprint sets may be carried in all police automobiles for just such occasions.

Although businesses must open for business at regular or designated times, the owner or manager should be requested to assist in police investigations, which includes the taking of prints where they are suspected to exist.

348. Taking photographs of crime scene.

Photographs present the details of a crime vividly and accurately, are valuable permanent records of the appearance of the crime scene or evidence, and present positive identification. The investigator should make a complete photographic record of the crime scene before anything is moved. Sufficient photographs of all aspects of the scene should be taken to show clearly all relevant evidential material. Exterior photographs should include an over-all view of the scene, including immediate surroundings; views of all entrances and exits of buildings; footprints or tire tracks and skid marks if pertinent to the case; property damage, including over-all scene and close-ups; and positions of all articles of evidence. When photographing interior crime scenes, the investigator should take overlapping photographs in a clockwise direction in order to cover the entire interior. These photographs should include all entrances and exits, the view of the room from the door, and high-angle and close-up views of all evidence, particularly fingerprints, documents, markings caused by forced entry or exit, indications of a struggle, and immovable evidence. Extremely high or low placement should be avoided unless there is a specific reason for such placement. The plane of film and of the subject, if possible, should be parallel, and the subject should be centered in the viewfinder. When possible, a tripod or other support should be utilized to minimize camera movement. In recording camera position, the investigator makes exact measurements from immovable objects on the scene to a plumb bob suspended from the camera or tripod head.

349. Maintaining chain of custody of evidence.

Each person who handles a piece of evidence from the time it is discovered until it has been properly disposed of is a link in the chain of custody. The chain of custody should be as limited as possible, and a complete record should be maintained by registering the date, time, names, and signatures each time the evidence changes hands. The chain of custody is maintained on the back of the evidence tag if used, or by copies of receipts issued each time the evidence is transferred. Each individual handling the evidence will request and obtain a receipt for the article when he relinquishes control of it. When the investigator delivers exposed film to a photographic laboratory for development and processing, he obtains a receipt from the technician. If exposed film is mailed, it should be registered and a return receipt requested. The technician places his identifying mark and case number on the clear edge of the negative and on the back of the final prints after the negatives are printed, and obtains a receipt when he returns the negatives and prints to the investigator. The investigator then places his identifying mark and case number on the negatives and prints, after which the photographs may be filed with the case history until needed.

350. Officers apprehend a suspect who states that he wants to talk and "get this thing off my chest."

A confession is a voluntary declaration by a person that he is guilty of a crime. It differs from an admission in that the confession is an express and complete acknowledgment of guilt of the crime, while an admission is merely an acknowledgment of some fact which tends to prove guilt. There is a distinct procedure for introducing confessions, which is that it must be given freely and voluntarily. The improper means used to obtain a confession may be summarized thusly: "A judge will admit a confession into evidence only if the defendant was not induced to make the statement (1) under compulsion or by infliction or threats of infliction of suffering upon him or another, or by prolonged interrogation under such circumstances as to render the statement involuntary, or (2) by threats or promises concerning action to be taken by a public official with reference to the crime, likely to cause the accused to make such a statement falsely, and made by a person whom the accused reasonably believed to have the power or authority to execute the same."

Under the Escobedo-Dorado-Miranda decisions all admissions and confessions resulting from interrogations must be preceded by appropriate warnings!

It is always good practice to have a witness present, have the confession reduced to writing, have each page read and initialed by the confessant, and include therein that it was given freely and voluntarily. Time, place, and date, including names of persons present, should be included.

351. All the victims of a check passer call in and report that they have received money orders from another state to cover the checks with a request to tear up the checks.

Once a crime has been committed there can be no compromise thereof, except when application to the court in specific instances. This situation does not fall within the compromise provisions of most state laws—hence the victims should be informed not to tear up the checks, but to make appropriate crime reports for possible criminal prosecution.

352. An officer is called to a large grocery store by the store manager, who has in custody a person whom he caught outside the store with several packages of frozen food inside his shirt.

If the suspect enters the store with the intent to commit a theft, he thereby commits the crime of burglary under most state laws. If these facts can be proven, the suspect should be arrested and booked for burglary, and a crime report for burglary should be obtained from the store manager.

If the intent with which the suspect entered the store cannot be proven, the crime is a petty theft, a misdemeanor. In this situation, the offense is obviously not committed in the presence of the officer, therefore, the arrest must be made by the store manager if he so desires. If no physical arrest is decided upon, the suspect may be proceeded against by making application for a complaint from the office of the prosecuting attorney. The latter situation is especially applicable in those states in which a "breaking and entering" is necessary to constitute a burglary.

353. An officer observes a radio, from which the manufacturer's serial number has been removed, displayed in a pawn broker's window.

These facts indicate that a misdemeanor has been committed by the possession of an article with a missing serial number. This is covered by state laws, which generally read:

"Purchase, possession or sale of certain articles from which serial number or identification mark has been removed:

"Any person who knowingly buys, sells, receives, disposes of, conceals, or has in his possession a radio, piano, phonograph, sewing machine, washing machine, typewriter, adding machine, comptometer, bicycle, a firearm, safe or vacuum cleaner, Dictaphone, watch, watch movement, watch case, or any mechanical or electrical device, appliance, contrivance, material, piece of apparatus or equipment, from which the manufacturer's name plate, serial number, or any other distinguishing mark has been removed, defaced, covered, altered, or destroyed, is guilty of a misdemeanor.

"This section does not apply to those cases or instances where any of the changes or alterations enumerated in the first paragraph have been customarily made or done as an established practice and regular conduct of business, by the original manufacturer or by his duly appointed representative, or under specific authorization from the original manufacturer."

354. A man approaches an officer in plain clothes, wanting him to act as a lookout while the man burglarizes a store. The officer consents, but in the meantime notifies his superiors who tell him to proceed as planned. However, the suspect changes the plan at the last minute, and he acts as lookout while the officer commits burglary. The suspect who is now acting as lookout is immediately arrested for burglary.

This generally is an erroneous booking, because no burglary is committed, since the officer did not enter with intent to commit a theft, but entered with only the intent to apprehend a suspect. The proper booking should be for "solicitation," which usually reads, in most states:

"Every person who solicits another to offer or accept or join in the offer or acceptance of a bribe, or to commit or join in the commission of murder, robbery, burglary, grand theft, receiving stolen property, extortion, rape by force and violence, perjury, subornation of perjury, forgery, or kidnapping, is punishable by imprisonment in the county jail not longer than one year or in the state prison not longer than five years, or by fine of not more than five thousand dollars. Such offense must be proved by the testimony of two witnesses, or of one witness and corroborating circumstances."

355. An officer answers a silent burglar alarm at a large retail fur store. On his arrival he checks entrances and discovers that the front door of the store is unlocked, but has been pulled shut.

Since this is a silent alarm, there is a good possibility that the burglar will still be inside the store. The officer should immediately radio for assistance so that all possible exits may be covered before search of the store is commenced. Upon arrival of additional officers, they should be stationed strategically, with at least one or two going to the roof or fire escape, if possible. After this is done, a search may be commenced. It may be advisable to first locate the light switches and turn on all the lights in the store, rather than conduct a search with only a flashlight. The owner should be notified and a report made of the incident.

356. An officer of a merchandising company complains to an officer that he has entrusted a large sum of money to an agent of the company to be used for a specific purpose, but that the agent has converted the money to his (the agent's) own use.

Such an act is usually considered embezzlement. It is prosecuted as a felony or misdemeanor, depending upon the value of the property taken. The officer should take a crime report, and handle it according to departmental regulations.

357. In investigating a ring of racketeers, an officer finds that the ring, while still operating, was investigated by another police agency. To gain information, an inquiry is made to the other police agency, and they deny any knowledge of the case.

In this situation, it is possible that the other agency may still be working on the case, and as every good policeman knows, it is sometimes better to maintain secrecy than to risk hampering an investigation. These facts, however, could be documented and a conference had with a county-wide or a state-wide police agency such as the prosecuting attorney's office or the Attorney General's office. Your investigation should continue.

358. While investigating a non-related case, an officer accidentally obtains conclusive evidence that certain city officials in the purchasing department are accepting kickbacks. The officer makes a report which is forwarded to higher officials. Time passes—and nothing is done.

There is nothing to prevent the officer from asking his superior to check on what is being done regarding the investigation of the alleged briberies. It is always a good policy to document important facts and these facts would seem to be of sufficient importance to justify documentation. If the matter is being handled exclusively by the department of the officer concerned, it would seem that nothing should be done to hamper the proper investigation to the successful conclusion of the case. If the matter is not being handled exclusively by the aforementioned department, it would seem that the office of the prosecuting attorney or Attorney General would be interested in receiving information regarding the facts. Good judgment will usually dictate what course of action to follow.

ANIMALS

359. An officer is informed that a citizen has found a lost animal.

The finder can legally retain the animal and attempt to locate the owner. However, the officer may advise the person that the retention of lost property without reasonable effort made to locate the owner could constitute theft.

Some departments provide that an officer receiving information regarding a found animal shall, without delay, notify the nearest humane society or pound. The notification shall include, if practicable, the name, address, and phone number of the person who has possession of the animal.

360. An officer finds a dead animal in the street.

Some cities provide that when dead animals are found in the street, the pound or humane society shall be notified. Field units may make such notification by radio to the communications control center operator.

In some situations, if wild animals such as a dead deer or elk are found, the carcass could be turned over to the Salvation Army or other charitable organization.

361. A person lost her valuable cocker spaniel and now desires to make a "lost report."

Many departments do not take lost animal reports, but instead, refer the person to the nearest animal shelter, humane society or pound. However, if the situation indicates that the animal had been stolen, then a theft report could be taken under the general rule that anything that can be identified and has some value can be the subject of theft. Good public relations dictate that the officer should assist insofar as may be feasible, and that he should probably file a report. The owner should be advised to call the department if the dog returns home.

362. A mother informs an officer that her three-year-old daughter was bitten by an animal.

If emergency treatment seems necessary, call an ambulance. If an ambulance is not available and departmental regulations permit, drive the mother and daughter to the nearest emergency hospital.

In any event, when an animal bites a person, a written report should be made, and a copy forwarded to the agency which handles rabies control, and should include the following information: (1) Name, address, telephone number, and age of the victim, (2) Name, address, and telephone number of the owner of the animal, (3) Description of the animal (breed, color, and sex), (4) Circumstances of the attack, (5) Nature of treatment, when and by whom given, (6) Location of the wound on the body, and (7) The date the bite occurred.

363. An officer is called to an area where a vicious or rabid animal is running loose.

If possible, the animal should be isolated and held for rabies observation. Call the humane society or pound for assistance. If it is necessary to shoot the animal to prevent injury to persons or children, the animal should be shot through the body and not through the head because the head is necessary in tests to determine if the animal is actually rabid.

364. A person complains that her six dogs have been poisoned in her back yard. Two of them are dead, and the others are sick.

This is a misdemeanor under most state laws which usually provide: "Every person who, without the consent of the owner, wilfully administers poison to any animal, the property of another, or exposes any substance, with the intent that the same shall be taken or swallowed by such animal, is guilty of a misdemeanor."

The person should be advised regarding the above law, and a crime report should be taken naming possible suspects. The person should be advised that it may be possible for the local animal shelter, humane society, or pound to make an autopsy to determine whether or not the dogs had actually been poisoned. It may also be advisable to preserve samples of the poisoned food for laboratory analysis. Officers could also contact neighbors in the area for similar instances.

Check your local ordinances regarding the legality of having six dogs in one yard.

365. An officer observes that several dogs are running loose in his patrol area.

This situation would not require police action, other than the police notifying the animal shelter of the existing violation of a city or county ordinance, which requires that dogs be confined to fenced areas or be on a leash. The animal shelter officers should make necessary reports and citations.

366. A woman complains that someone stole her cocker spaniel, she thinks. She wants something done about it.

Dogs and other animals which can be identified as belonging to someone can be the subject of theft. If the circumstances indicate that a theft has occurred, a crime report should be taken. It would seem, however, that before the report is taken some preliminary investigation should be made such as calling the local humane societies or dog pounds. Whether there has been a felony or misdemeanor committed would depend on the value of the dog.

367. A person complains to an officer that a neighbor's dog barks constantly.

Most cities and counties have ordinances pertaining to barking dogs, crowing roosters, and other bothersome noises caused by animals. In this situation, however, it would seem that the officer's role should be that of mediator. Hence the officer should obtain a complete story from the complaining citizen and then contact the owner of the dog and advise him of the complaint and explain to both parties the law in the situation. Both parties should also be advised that if the situation is not remedied a complaint could then be sought from the office of the prosecuting attorney for a criminal prosecution. If the owner is not at home, leave a note with the time, nature of the complaint, the officer's name and number, and his division of assignment. Record the event in notebook or daily log.

368. An officers answers a disturbance of the peace call and finds that one citizen is holding another because the former's dog has just been run over by the auto of the detained citizen.

Generally, there are city and county ordinances prohibiting dogs from running at large, in which case the owner of the dog may be proceeded against by application of complaint for allowing his dog to run loose. As far as the dog being run over is concerned, such action is not in violation of any law, unless it is done deliberately. If the action was deliberate, it would be considered malicious mischief. If no crime is proven, it could be suggested to the parties concerned that they should consult with their respective lawyers for any possible civil litigation, after which the officer should make a regular report of the incident and turn it in to the department.

369. In response to many calls at the complaint board officers find a barking dog inside a house with no one at home at 3:00 a.m. The dog is at an opened but screened window and is still barking.

Chances are the officers will be bitten if an attempt is made to force open the screened window. If a person is available from the pound or humane society who is adept at handling such cases he may be called so that the dog may be taken into protective custody to be held for his owner. If such a person is not available it is suggested that the officers make some attempt to close the window and thus diminish the noise from the barking of the dog. In this situation the officers could leave a note for the owner to call the station regarding the disturbance and when the persons call the desk officer could inform them regarding the possibility of a complaint being secured against them for allowing such a disturbance to occur.

There seems to be no law setting forth what the officers should do in this situation except the law of practicality and the above suggestions are aimed at achieving this. Of course, the officer should not ignore the possibility of a violation of a law governing cruelty to animals, such as leaving the dog without food and water for an unusual period.

370. An officer finds an animal injured in the street, and it seems necessary to destroy it.

When a sick or injured animal is found on the street the nearest animal shelter or humane society should be notified immediately. Units in the field may make this notification by means of radio to the communication control operator. If the animal shelter or humane society is unavailable and it seems necessary to remove the animal from the street, the officer can use the police car for conveying the animal to the proper place if practicable. If the animal is too large or is seriously injured, some attempt should be made to locate the owner. Children in the neighborhood are usually a good source of information regarding the home of a pet. When all else fails, attempt to secure witnesses to the incident prior to destroying it with your service revolver, because an owner of a pet may feel that such action was not necessary.

When shooting, exercise care that the bullet does not ricochet. If there is any indication that the animal may be rabid, destroy it by shooting elsewhere than in the head.

FEDERAL OFFENSES

371. Upon interviewing a suspect, an officer discovers that the person is in violation of a federal crime, whereupon the suspect is arrested and taken to the local jail for booking.

Peace officers have the legal authority to arrest for federal crimes. The suspect is booked and kept at the local jail until he can be presented for trial in a federal court. Generally, upon the arrest of a person for a federal violation, the local office of the Federal Bureau of Investigation, or concerned federal agency, is contacted and given the facts and circumstances. In some situations, such as for violations of the Selective Service Act, and illegal wearing of a service uniform, the approval of the local office of the FBI must be obtained prior to the booking of the arrestee. In such cases, the name of the FBI agent approving the arrest and booking should appear on the arrest report. (See Appendix D.)

372. An officer answers a drunk call and finds the drunk in a federal post office.

If the property is exclusively federal property, the arrest must be made under an appropriate federal law, because state and local laws do not apply to federal property which is exclusively under the control of the federal government. The officer should check with the prosecuting attorney for information as to whether jurisdiction has been ceded by the federal government back to the local government, so that state or local laws would be applicable, in which case the arrest could be made under the laws of the latter.

373. An officer has the fact brought to his attention that a civilian walking down the sidewalk, and still within sight, is wearing unauthorized items of a military uniform.

The illegal wearing of a uniform is generally both a violation of a state law and the federal law. Departmental policies will dictate as to which law the person should be booked under. Generally, if the person is arrested under the federal law, the local office of the Federal Bureau of Investigation is usually notified before a booking is made.

374. An officer stops a possible stolen vehicle. It is ascertained that it is not stolen, but a passenger is an "AWOL" sailor. The sailor refuses to go with the officer or wait for the shore patrol.

Generally, arrests for "AWOL" military personnel are not made by civil law enforcement officers unless authorized by the military headquarters in the area. The officer should have the military headquarters contacted for authority to arrest and detain the "AWOL." In the southern California area the headquarters at Fort MacArthur, Office of the Provost Marshal, San Pedro, California, has issued a statement of policy which is quoted as follows:

"The apprehension and return to military control of military personnel reported AWOL and/or Desertion, by civil law enforcement officers, will be confined to those military personnel for whom WD AGO Forms 45 have been issued, or military personnel whose apprehension has been specifically requested by competent military authority."

375. In stopping a car for a traffic violation, an officer finds that the owner-driver has possibly entered the United States illegally.

Under federal immigration laws, the illegal entry is a federal misdemeanor for which the person may be arrested at any time, because it is considered a continuing misdemeanor. The officer should perform at least four actions:

(1) Write the citation. (2) Arrest the person and book "Enroute Immigration." (3) Impound the car for safekeeping, and (4) Make appropriate reports.

376. An officer stops a covered stake truck for a traffic violation. Upon talking to the driver, he finds that there are several persons in the truck who may have entered the country illegally.

The officer should write the citation if the violation so demands. The foreigners should then be checked for possible illegal entry. If there are any in the country illegally, then the persons concerned should be arrested for illegal entry, a misdemeanor. In this situation, it may be that the driver of the truck is a party to the illegal entry and if so, he should be arrested as a principal to the illegal entry. If there is any doubt as to the driver's participation in the illegal entry, he should be released and application for complaint sought from the office of the prosecuting attorney.

377. An officer is approached by a man waving a ten dollar bill. The man states that the bill is counterfeit. The officer looks at the bill and is uncertain whether or not it is genuine.

The Secret Service and banks are the best qualified persons on the subject of counterfeit money. Hence the person should be directed to the nearest office of that agency. If that office does not have an agency in the vicinity, the person should be directed to the station, where the bill could be examined with a magnifying glass. There are many telltale items on counterfeit bills which will indicate that they are counterfeit, such as indistinct lettering and blurred points on the edges of the United States seal. These items can be readily distinguished under magnification. If the bill is determined to be a counterfeit, it should be booked as evidence and a crime report taken from the victim, especially noting where he got the bill, description of the person who gave it to him, etc. Meanwhile, an agent of the Secret Service could be contacted by telephone regarding the incident, so that appropriate action could be taken by the federal officers.

378. Numerous complaints concerning TV interference are received from the same neighborhood. It is believed to be caused by a nearby ham radio operator.

Complaints of this nature are usually referred to the Federal Communications Commission. Before calling the FCC, however, it may be suggested to the parties that the ham operator be contacted and told that his radio is causing interference. If this fails, then a complaint should be made to the FCC for appropriate action by that agency.

379. A detective observes a man in a post office break a chain and take a ball-point pen and put it in his pocket.

The detective should place the man under arrest and take him to the person in charge of the post office and relate what happened. This may be a jurisdictional matter, and the detective should be guided accordingly. If the post office is exclusively federal property, then the prosecution must be had under the appropriate federal laws, and the person prosecuted in the federal court. If the post office is not on land which is under the exclusive jurisdiction of the federal government, then state and local laws could be used for a prosecution. The person in charge of the post office should be able to give this necessary information so that the officer may proceed accordingly.

PERSONNEL PROBLEMS

380. A sergeant is called aside by an officer who informs him that upon answering a burglary call, his partner picked up a bottle of liquor at the scene and put it in the trunk of the radio car.

The sergeant should call both officers aside and ask the partner regarding his actions in picking up the bottle. After receiving the stories from both officers, the sergeant should take the bottle and order the officers to the station. At the station, written reports should be obtained from both parties. At this point, departmental policy and rules will dictate whether or not the officer would be arrested for theft. Some departments require that designated superior officers be contacted at home before arresting an officer.

381. An officer arrests a drunk. In the station it is determined that he is a police officer.

Police officers have no immunity from drunk arrests or any other type of arrest. However, some departments have policies which provide that the officer shall be taken home by a supervisor after having his identification and gun removed from his possession. In such cases the officer is usually directed to appear at the office of the chief of police the next day for disciplinary action. Usually the disciplinary action is more severe than if the person had merely posted and forfeited bail as an ordinary drunk can do. It is suggested that the departmental policy be spelled out for the proper answer to this situation.

382. An experienced officer working a plainclothes patrol car is assigned to work with a newly assigned partner. The experienced officer stops the car in front of an apartment house and tells his partner to wait in the car while he visits his girl friend in the apartment house. Forty-five minutes later the younger partner hears a radio call for his unit to report to the station.

The officer should make an attempt to get his partner before reporting to the station. If the officer is unable to locate his partner, he should proceed to the station without him. In the latter case, a relating of the facts to a superior officer should make it possible for the superior to take appropriate remedial action. If the officer was able to secure his partner before reporting to the station, it is suggested that the younger officer inform the "old timer" that such actions will not be tolerated, and that there are possibly better ways for a person to spend his lunch or dinner time. If no cooperation is secured, the younger officer should ask for another partner.

383. An officer persists in wearing a dirty uniform. You warn him but he does nothing to correct the situation. What further action?

Dirty or unkempt uniforms certainly do nothing to enhance the image of the officer in the eyes of the public. Consequently this officer should receive constructive disciplinary action or, failing this, suspension or removal from office.

384. An officer at the scene of a fire is told by a bystander that one of the firemen is drunk.

Firemen and policemen are handled differently from ordinary drunks, because it is considered more serious for an officer or a fireman to appear drunk in public. Therefore, the following suggested procedures could be used:
  1. Obtain the name and address of the witness and ask how he arrived at his conclusion.
  2. Have the fireman identified and contact his superior for witnessing.
  3. Check his sobriety.
  4. If in doubt, take him to the hospital for a medical examination.
  5. If the doctors concur on the drunkenness, arrest him or release him to the custody of his superiors.
  6. Make appropriate written reports.

385. A tenant in an apartment house reports a mink coat stolen while another apartment is on fire. She thinks a fireman took it.

The preliminary investigation should include an inquiry as to why she makes the particular accusation. An appropriate crime report should be taken for theft and all the facts related therein. The preliminary investigation should also include a thorough search of the area, including a search of the parked cars and the fire apparatus. During the search, the fireman's superior should be present, because he is in charge of the fire equipment and personnel.

386. A private citizen complains to an officer that she just came from a firehouse and that when she asked for a fire permit, the fireman used obscene language to her, which would constitute a disturbance of the peace.

Sometimes false accusations are made when a person has been denied some request. It is advisable to ask the citizen whether or not she secured the fire permit, and what was the reason for its denial, if such was the case. At this point, it is sometimes advisable to warn the person that making a false report is a misdemeanor. If the officer is satisfied that the citizen's complaint is a valid one, the officer could either advise the citizen to present her case to the prosecuting attorney or he could take a disturbance of the peace report, or he could advise the citizen to report the incident to the fire chief. In any event, the officer should make a written report, followed by an interdepartmental communication to the fire department.

387. While working the early morning watch, an officer's partner drives into the hills, crawls into the back seat, and goes to sleep.

An officer who covers up for another officer usually assumes the penalties which would attach to the latter's wrongdoing. While this is not a hard and fast rule, it is one which is usually used by most departments. Another consideration is that a person who persists in sleeping on city time is not doing his job at all. This means that when he reaches for his pay check, he is obtaining money under false pretenses, but this fact would probably not suffice for a criminal prosecution. A practical solution to this would seem to be that this type of action will not be tolerated, and he had better climb back into the front seat and continue patrol. If the partner persists in staying in the back seat, the car should be driven to the station, a supervisor notified, and a request made for an alert partner.

389. One of the officers under your supervision is not doing his work. You call the man in private, and tell him that you expect him to carry his part of the load, whereupon he complains to the chief of police that you are "riding" him because of a prejudice.

In dealing with personnel problems, it is almost always wise to document the situations as they arise. By this method, a person's work record will speak for itself. The written reports should indicate whether or not there is prejudice or mere "wolf calling," although it is sometimes very difficult to pass judgment on when a person is or is not meeting the desired standards of the department, yet the supervisor must use his best judgment in evaluation of the worth of a person as compared with others performing similar work. It would also seem that the supervisor's judgment may be improved by placing the officer in a position where the work could be evaluated objectively and where he could be expected to improve his performance record. In any event, it would seem that documentation would be desirable for later possible reference.

390. After two officers have been working together for some time, officer

"A" confides in officer "B" that he has been betting on the horses and suggests that they work together as "bookies."

The growing professionalization of peace officers demands not only legal but ethical conduct. In fact, many police departments, such as the New York Police Department, have adopted strict codes of ethics which call for exemplary conduct beyond that expected of the general citizenry. Becoming more specific, bookmaking is generally classified as a felony, hence this situation demands that a full report be made of the incident to the immediate supervisor, who will then be in a position to take appropriate action. Naturally, the question of loyalty is involved—such as that which exists between partners, between subordinates, and superiors, between all personnel and to the department, and one's loyalty to one's own integrity and family. Since it is impossible to evaluate the characters of the parties concerned by this discussion, it is suggested that there is no room for unethical persons in law enforcement.

391. Officers on patrol observe a passing parade and a band playing the National Anthem.

1. The Flag
    On approach of the flag, officers in uniform (with hat on) will face the flag and render a military salute.
    In civilian clothes, he should stand at attention, remove his hat and place it (or his hand) over his left breast.
2. The National Anthem
    When the National Anthem is played, officers shall stand at attention and, if in uniform, shall render a military salute.
    When in a motor vehicle, the vehicle shall come to a stop and the driver should sit at attention. All passengers should alight and stand at attention.

392. The partner of an officer confides that he had been working narcotics and still has a few narcotics in his locker. He suggests a partnership to sell the contraband.

A person of this character should be operated as you would an ordinary crook. The better procedure would seem to be to report these facts to a superior officer so that there would be no chance of a slipup in carrying this case to a successful arrest and prosecution.

393. You have men working for two hours after you go off watch. It comes to your attention that they go off the air one hour early; go home early. What action?

This would probably be a good opportunity for exercising functional supervision, which means that supervisors on the other watch should be contacted for their assistance in checking on such activities. The latter would be exercising functional supervision of line officers, which is one of the permissible deviations from line command supervision. Of course, the officers should thereafter be asked to explain such actions on their parts so that remedial and/or appropriate disciplinary action can be taken.

394. Two officers are assigned to a specific car on the early morning watch in uniform patrol. One of the officers observes that the other officer is intoxicated.

The intoxicated officer should be removed from duty immediately. He should be driven to the station and the sergeant in charge should be informed of the situation. Departmental procedure will dictate the procedure to be followed from this point on but generally an officer in an intoxicated condition has his badge, cap piece and other identification, and his gun removed from his person. He is then usually driven home by a sergeant and ordered to return to the station the next morning at 9:00 a.m. for disciplinary action.

395. A police officer arrests a felon and discovers that a reward had been posted for this subject's arrest. What steps should he follow, if any?

If rewards are allowed to be received by your department, the officer concerned should make a formal written narration of the event, and include a request that the reward be distributed according to the departmental regulations. If your department prohibits the collection of rewards, no attempt should be made to circumvent departmental orders. Usually department policies provide that all rewards should be paid into a pension or welfare fund.

396. A supervisor receives reliable information that an officer has made a personal loan of $100 from an unsavory character with a criminal record.

Officers should remain above suspicion which means that an officer should not engage in any activity which would hamper law enforcement work or tend to embarrass the department. Consorting with hoods, racketeers, or suspects should not be practiced unless an arrest is contemplated.

In this situation, the supervisor should discuss the ramifications of such an action by the officer. If the discussion reveals good faith or an honest mistake on the part of the officer, no further action would seem necessary. When the judgment of the officer is questionable, some sort of documentation by way of making a written report for the next immediate supervisor would seem to be in order.

397. What controls should be instituted in order to attain equal work standards, and uniform operating procedures on all watches?

It is not possible to establish either equal working standards or uniform operating procedures, except in a general way. Sometimes officers may write more tickets during the daytime rush hours than officers would write between midnight and eight in the morning. Also, laws and court decisions vary in their right of the officers to stop a person in the daytime as contrasted with nighttime. In spite of these variations it is possible to check on the relative efficiency of officers by having a roving sergeant in a patrol car checking on field operations, together with the utilization of tabulations of "called for service," pinmaps, and statistics. In the final analysis, however, it is not the mere number of arrests that are made, but the type of judgment which is being exercised by the officers and the relative amount of crime in each assigned area.

398. You report to a new division or watch as a new sergeant and find that you are the only one on duty with rank, all others are officers and roll-call is about to begin. The captain, lieutenant, and other sergeants are on days off or on vacation. How do you proceed?

Secure the assistance of a senior officer. It is not expected that new supervisors will know all the answers; nor is it expected that an officer cannot benefit from the experience of others. Hence, it would seem not only necessary, but appropriate, to enlist the aid of those officers who may contribute toward the efficiency of the department. The mere fact that a senior officer is consulted is a recognition that he has a wealth of background experience that may be tapped.

399. What, if anything, would be done about the officer who is a chronic "griper" especially to the other officers with whom he works?

It seems that we could ask this officer for a list of his gripes, upon the premise that they may be justified. Secondly, it would seem appropriate to sit down with him and listen—a "hearing him out." At this point the gripes can be analyzed with him in a cooperative effort to establish or reconcile their validity.

400. You are reading a new order to the watch and an old-timer says "BS" to every sentence. What action?

He should be called in and asked "why?" Generally, an old-timer is either an informal leader or can be an informal leader. With this in mind he could be challenged to meet the test of a leader, so that instead of being considered a constant griper he can contribute considerably to the solidarity of the watch. This means that he could be consulted prior to the reading of the new orders to the watch and obtain his reaction. It has been found that the newer officers are reluctant to ask for an explanation during the roll call, but wait until after the roll call is over and then proceed to ask someone with more experience what the order meant.

401. A traffic officer stops pretty girls and talks to them too much and too long. What action?

All such problems must be accompanied by a question to the officer as to "why?" To stop and talk to a girl is not consistent with good police work unless it is a valid function, such as issuing a warning or a traffic ticket— these only occupy three or four minutes and anything longer should be questioned. It does not make any difference if there is any complaint, because it is the supervisor's job to see that those under his command are performing accurately, efficiently, and with good judgment.

402. You are a sergeant. One of the men on your watch invites you and your wife over for dinner next Saturday night. You know the officer quite well, but only on the job. What do you do?

It is nice to be friendly, and it is encouraging to know that a sergeant is liked by a subordinant. But it must be borne in mind that this may be a bid for preferential treatment. Good judgment will detect the motivation behind the invitation and the sergeant can act accordingly.

403. What should you do as the superior officer of an officer who is accused of theft by a drunk the officer is booking?

Drunks may be fairly rational at times, which means that such accusations should be investigated. If the item which is alleged to have been taken is identifiable, the supervising officer should consider an immediate search. If the item is not identifiable, a follow-up investigation would probably be better. In such cases another officer, working undercover, could pose as a drunk with some marked items on him. The courts have ruled that such "setting of traps" does not amount to entrapment but is merely affording an opportunity for a person to commit a crime. If the accused is guilty of theft, he should be arrested and taken to court just as any other thief should be handled.

404. What should you do as the superior officer of an officer whom you see unloading groceries from the police unit to his own car just after he comes off watch?

Department policy will dictate whether an officer will shop on his lunch hour, this would also apply to such things as obtaining a hair cut on one's lunch break. Most departments proceed on the theory that such actions might be misunderstood and hold that the officer should not perform any action during his tour of duty which would be considered personal in nature.

405. What answer would you give an officer who complains that his wife wants him to work days?

The policy of the department comes first. Some departments permit officers to trade watches with other officers so that in this problem it would be possible for him to satisfy his wife's desires. In such cases, however, if he is not successful in finding another officer to trade watches with him he would have no alternative but to work his assigned watch, resign from the department, or change his wife's attitude.

406. You are patrolling the "lovers' lane" area at night and see a car parked near some bushes. Upon checking with a flashlight, you see an officer in uniform embracing a policewoman in uniform. What should you do?

The personal off-duty activities of an officer are not generally of any concern to a department, except when such actions reflect detrimentally on the department. The officer should be called in and advised that even though he has a personal life of his own the mere fact that he is wearing a uniform carries with it the implication that he is on duty—at least in the eyes of a civilian. He should also be advised that all officers should "not only avoid evil, but should avoid the appearance of evil."

407. As sergeant, what would you do about a complaint from a loan company that an officer on your watch is not paying his bills?

As in all of these problems, you should obtain the officer's version of the situation. It may be possible that the complainant has a legitimate cause to plea, but the loan company should be advised, most emphatically, that the police department is not a collection agency. The officer should be given assistance in helping achieve a satisfactory solution to his problem.

408. You receive word that one of your officers is greatly in debt and isn't meeting his obligations. What actions?

Normally, the private life of an officer should not be the concern of the department. The exceptions would be where his actions are such as to bring discredit to the department. It would seem appropriate to get his side of the story and consider the possibility of coercion or enmity before taking any action. Since this is not an emergency situation, a written report can be obtained from the officer and forwarded to the commanding officer for his consideration and action.

409. You are on duty as a Watch Commander and the Lieutenant comes to work drunk and in uniform. What should you do? What report?

Appropriate drunk tests should be given for later prosecution and dismissal from the department. Following this, his badge and weapon should be removed, including any other personal property, before booking him for being drunk in public. Of course, appropriate written reports should be made on all actions taken.

410. You are on patrol with another Sergeant and answer a burglary call to a liquor store. The other Sergeant takes a bottle of whisky and puts it in the police car. What action? What reports?

Many actions can be taken, but first ask him why he picked it up. It might be that he has some reason to believe that it may have fingerprints of the burglar. Also, it may be that he is a thief, or he may have had prior permission from the owner of the liquor store to take a bottle of liquor. If there is any indication that the officer is merely taking advantage of the situation, the car should be driven to the station immediately for a report to the commanding officer prior to the booking of the officer for theft.

411. You notice that an officer is having trouble with a motorist who is receiving a traffic citation. The citizen complains to you that the officer has been drinking and that he won't sign the ticket. What do you do?

All complaints of private persons must be listened to and investigated. This means that the officer must be checked to verify a complaint. If the private person's complaint is valid, it would seem that the officer should be relieved of duty and taken to the station for appropriate disciplinary action. In each case the name and address of the person, plus a statement of his complaint, should be made a matter of record so that the party may either be subpoenaed as a witness and/or informed of the action that was taken. In the event the private person's complaint is not substantiated he should be advised to sign the citation or be placed under arrest in accordance with the laws of the state concerned. In any event a written record should be made of the incident.

412. You have an officer who fails to write any traffic tickets. You explain how to write a ticket and he writes a few but then doesn't write any more. What should you do?

The lack of training or improper attitude would probably account for such an action. One of the first steps would be to ask the officer his reason for failing to perform an important part of his duties. In the larger department it is possible to put square pegs in square holes because there are a vast number of assignments which can be made. In the smaller departments, however, each officer is a "generalist" rather than a specialist; which means that all officers must perform all functions. When any officer is lacking in ability or attitude to perform the duties required of him, there is no alternative but to terminate him from the department.

MISCELLANEOUS

413. Ugly rumors are circulating concerning minority groups, such as— that a Negro has raped a white woman, and another—that a white man has killed a Negro without reason.

People, even those who are usually sensible, can go hog-wild when they hear a rumor.

A police officer, though, must not. He is a trained, professional man and his job is keeping the peace.

1. The only antidote for poisonous rumor is fact. Get the facts promptly and circulate them as widely as possible. Get in touch with the local newspaper(s), radio station(s), civic organizations, and minority group organizations and give them all the facts.

2. Do not repeat a rumor outside of official police circles.

3. Question the tale-bearer and insist upon verification and proof. Make it plain to this person the implications of his actions, and what they could lead to. Stopping a rumor at any point can be of great significance in shortening its range.

Once the immediate problem has been settled, look at the larger picture. Was this a single crackpot rumor or have there been quite a number of them lately? Is everything normal or do you feel something is brewing? You should regard these incidents as a doctor would a temperature. Very often, a little too much sun will create a temporary fever. But sometimes a rising temperature is a warning signal that the patient is sick.

All rumors should be reported to superior officers. They are in an even better position to assess the danger-potential of rumors in the community and, in addition, can take immediate steps to further counteract these rumors before the peace of the community is jeopardized.

414. An officer witnesses a inter-ethnic conflict—a potential cause of a riot.

Once such event is related in a publication *With Justice for All* and is reprinted herewith by special permission from the Anti-Defamation League of B'nai B'rith:

Here's the true story of a young police officer who came up against a tough situation while he was, so to speak, still wet behind the ears.

It was about three in the morning, shortly after World War II, and this patrolman was walking his beat in New York's Harlem. It's the practice in New York, as it is in most of the big cities around the country, to give the newest men a go at the toughest assignments (critical areas) on the theory that their reflexes are in A-1 order, they can move fast and they have to learn fast.

As the patrolman stood in front of a bar-and-grill in the predominantly Negro neighborhood, a white Navy petty officer came out of a subway entrance and, lurching slightly, headed for the tavern. He obviously had already had more than he could hold.

The patrolman stepped into his path and began making friendly conversation. "Are you lost, bud?" he asked. As he related the incident later, he said, "I really had no right stopping him—he was free to go anywhere he wanted, and he could just as well have told me to go to hell. But he was drunk, and I felt no good would come of his going into that bar." The

Navy man allowed that maybe he did get off at the wrong subway stop, but so long as he was here, he'd just as soon go in and get a drink.

At this point a young Negro woman walked by. The Navy man leered at her and called out, "Hey nigger—want to join me?" The woman ignored him and walked abruptly into the bar.

"What did you want to do that for?" the patrolman asked angrily. "She wasn't bothering you—that could start real trouble!" This must have penetrated the alcoholic haze, for the Navy man began mumbling an apology. Then the door of the bar opened, and the same young woman walked out, in company with a Negro soldier. They approached the two men, and the soldier addressed himself to the policeman.

"Officer, this man has just insulted my wife."

Immediately, the patrolman said, "He sure did—I heard it myself. If you want to press charges, I'll take him in. But he's already sorry about the whole thing." The Navy man mumbled his apology again.

"No, I don't want to press charges. Forget it." The G. I. walked off with his wife, then had an afterthought and came back.

"Tell me, officer," he asked quietly, "what would have been the outcome if I were white and he were Negro?" He smiled wryly, rejoined his wife, and walked off.

It was a very good question, but one we'll leave for the sociologists to answer—here we're concerned with police work. And as police work, this patrolman's handling of a potentially dangerous situation couldn't be improved upon. He didn't have time to analyze it—he acted by instinct alone, and when it was over, he wiped the sweat off his brow and continued on his beat.

But let's analyze it:

He smelled danger and moved in.

He held the troublemaker to account without regard to the color of his skin.

He took firm and positive action when it was necessary.

There you have the essence of good professional police work:

a) going to the source of the trouble
b) being completely fair
c) acting decisively.

415. An officer observes a crowd or mob forming for the apparent purpose of staging a riot.

When a crowd or mob forms the experienced police officer will size it up and act fast.

1. If the crowd is still collecting, he can make a quick determination of the facts and take the involved parties into custody. This can sharply cut down the size of the crowd and prevent an incident from getting out of hand.

2. If a mob has already formed, call for reinforcements. Here a show of force is necessary, but not the use of force. Tension in a mob is usually highest at a point front and center. Look for the trouble-makers—and most excited individuals. Extricate these individuals.

3. A public address system can be a great help in dispersing a mob. The blare of the speaker, reinforced by a tone of authority, will catch and hold individual attention and turn it away from the excitable influences in the mob.

4. A police cordon around a dangerous area will keep curiosity seekers out and thus prevent them from being infected by mob psychosis.

Those are the "do's."

Here are the "don'ts":

1. Don't allow the antagonists to be near each other; separate them and let them cool off.

2. Don't show any partiality in any manner.

3. Don't make indiscriminate or mass arrests.

4. Above all—don't allow yourself to get excited in any manner. The police officer must be the one calm and neutralizing element, or his usefulness is nil.*

416. An ambulance and radio unit respond to a "heart attack" call. They find that an elderly man is suffering from a heart attack. He is a pensioner without friends, relatives, or money. It is necessary to keep administering oxygen to keep him alive. He refuses to go to a hospital and you know that a private hospital will not accept him without funds.

Any time a person's life is in danger an emergency situation exists. Emergency situations authorize an offier to take the person to an emergency hospital for appropriate treatment. If such is done it will then be the responsibility of the emergency hospital doctor to provide the necessary medication and care which may be available under the circumstances. In this situation it would be considered the officer's duty to take the person to the hospital even without his consent, because his life is in danger.

417. Upon answering an "unknown trouble" call, the officer finds a pregnant woman alone at home, and she seems too ill to care for herself.

Proper action to take depends upon whether the woman is ill or is about to deliver a child. If she is merely ill, her own doctor may be called by the officer, and her husband, relative or friend be informed regarding the situation in order that someone may take care of her. But when it appears that maternity service may be necessary, the officer should telephone for that particular doctor requested by the expectant mother. If no maternity service

---

* Reprinted with special permission from *With Justice for All* by the Anti-Defamation League of B'nai B'rith.

is readily available, then the city or county ambulance should be requested, especially when:

1. The woman's water has broken, or
2. There is bleeding, accompanied with labor pains, or
3. The labor pains are three to eight minutes apart and last one-half to one minute.

If the ambulance is late in arriving, secure the services of a female neighbor, or a person experienced in such situations.

418. A patrol officer is stopped by a person who requests that he push his car because the battery is dead.

This incident will normally be regulated by departmental policy and if this type of action is forbidden by departmental regulations, the officer should radio for a tow truck for assistance for the citizen.

If traffic conditions permit, check for the meeting of the bumpers so that damage to each car will not occur, and a simple push might prevent a potential traffic hazard. An officer should not push a stalled car on foot because of possible injury to himself.

419. An officer stops a speeding car and the driver states that his pregnant wife in the back seat is about to deliver a baby.

The solution to this problem is dependent upon two things: the time element and what the husband wishes to do. If the husband wishes to continue to a hospital, the officer should not detain him, but should escort him to the hospital. If the wife seems about to deliver, the officer could radio for an ambulance to meet them en route to the hospital by giving the route of travel. In this situation the husband should then follow the police vehicle. If the birth is in progress, an ambulance should be requested immediately and then assistance should be given to the husband in the delivery of the child. If the husband does not know what to do, then the officer should attempt to make the wife as comfortable as possible pending the arrival of the ambulance.

420. An officer answers a call where it is found that a six-year-old girl is choking on a bone. No ambulance is available.

Radio headquarters and notify them of the seriousness of the incident and request that a doctor stand by at your destination. Hold the child upside down and slap her on the back and if this is not immediately successful, take the child and a parent to the nearest emergency hospital, or private hospital. During the trip, hold the child head downward and with your finger attempt to dislodge the bone, providing that this might be accomplished without danger of further injury.

421. A detective is assigned to the auto theft detail. He goes to the prosecuting attorney's office and asks for a criminal complaint for "grand theft

auto" on a suspect. **The prosecuting attorney refuses to issue the complaint. The detective feels that he has a good case.**

Departmental policy dictates what action to take in such a case. It may be possible to have your superior talk to the prosecuting attorney. In extreme cases, the superior could authorize the presentation of the case to a judge or the county grand jury. In the interest of good harmony, it would seem that the matter should be discussed between members of the department and the prosecuting attorney's office before proceeding further. If a complaint is not forthcoming from the prosecuting attorney's office, a complete report should be made on the incident.

422. A detective goes to a preliminary hearing in court as the investigating officer of a burglary case. The defendant is in court, but the victim, who has been subpoenaed, does not show up to testify.

The prosecuting attorney should ask for a postponement so that the victim could be located. At this point, the judge could be requested to issue a warrant of arrest for contempt of court for failure to appear as a witness. It would seem that the officer has performed his duties and further action rests with the prosecuting attorney and the court.

APPENDICES

APPENDIX A

LAW ENFORCEMENT CODE OF ETHICS

AS A LAW ENFORCEMENT OFFICER, my fundamental duty is to serve mankind; to safeguard lives and property; to protect the innocent against deception, the weak against oppression or intimidation, and the peaceful against violence or disorder; and to respect the Constitutional rights of all men to liberty, equality and justice.

I will keep my private life unsullied as an example to all; maintain courageous calm in the face of danger, scorn, or ridicule; develop self-restraint; and be constantly mindful of the welfare of others. Honest in thought and deed in both my personal and official life, I will be exemplary in obeying the laws of the land and the regulations of my department. Whatever I see or hear of a confidential nature or that is confided to me in my official capacity will be kept ever secret unless revelation is necessary in the performance of my duty.

I will never act officiously or permit personal feelings, prejudices, animosities, or friendships to influence my decisions. With no compromise for crime and with relentless prosecution of criminals, I will enforce the law courteously and appropriately without fear or favor, malice or ill will, never employing unnecessary force or violence and never accepting gratuities.

I recognize the badge of my office as a symbol of public faith, and I accept it as a public trust to be held so long as I am true to the ethics of the police service. I will constantly strive to achieve these objectives and ideals, dedicating myself before God to my chosen profession . . . law enforcement.

ABOUT YOUR CITY

CITY OF . . . .

The city was officially incorporated as a (general law) (chartered) city on . . . . It encompasses an area of . . . . . . square miles, and has . . . . . . miles of improved streets.
(date)

The official population of the city, as of . . . . . ., is . . . . . ., based on a (special) (regular) census taken by . . . .
(date)
(agency)

There are . . . . . . public schools in the city; . . . . . . high schools; and . . . . . . elementary schools. In addition there (is) (are) . . . . . . parochial high school(s), and . . . . . . elementary parochial school(s). Approximately . . . . . . children attend these schools.

Essentially, the city is a . . . . community. Its
(residential, industrial, etc.)
current assessed valuation is $ . . . . Its current gross income is approximately $ . . . ., and its total operating budget is approximately $ . . . .

ORGANIZATION

The city has a . . . . type government. Responsi-
(i.e., council manager)
bility for general policy decisions with the city rests with the . . . ., who are elected. Their terms of office are . . . . . .
(i.e., council)
years.

The . . . . serves as general administrator for the
(i.e., city manager)
city. He is responsible to the . . . . While he serves he
(i.e., council)
has responsibility for the execution of all policies. All department heads are responsible to . . . . and work under his direction.

178

The city consists of the following departments:

....
....
....

In addition, it has the following agencies:

....
....
....

PERSONNEL RULES AND REGULATIONS: PAY AND WELFARE INFORMATION

All city employees are governed by the rules and regulations set forth by the ....,[1] which have been approved by the City Council. Recruitment, promotions, and appealable disciplinary actions are implemented in accordance with the .... rules and regulations.
(i.e., commission)
The .... consists of ...... members appointed for
(i.e., commission)
staggered terms of ...... years each, by the ...., and
(i.e., council)
they may be removed only for malfeasance in office.

Applicants for new positions or for promotions must file an application with the .... Examinations are sched-
(i.e., commission)
uled, and conducted by the ....
(examining agency)

Probationary Period

The probationary period for all new employees is ...... (months) (years), except that uniformed employees of the police and fire departments shall serve a probationary period of ...... year(s). The promotional probationary period is ...... months.

Medical Examinations

Complete medical examinations as prescribed by ....
(i.e., commission)

---

[1] Civil Service Commission, Personnel Advisory Council, etc.

are required for all new employees. Uniformed personnel are required to have . . . . medical examinations as prescribed,
(period)
and all other employees a . . . . physical check up. Such
(period)
examinations shall be conducted by the City at no expense to the employee.

Hours of Employment

All city employees are required to work a . . . . . . hour week. Working hours shall normally be from . . . . . . to . . . . . ., with a . . . . . . lunch period for all general service employees. Uniformed personnel are required to work shifts as prescribed by the departments. Fire department personnel shall work a . . . . . . hour day, ... days per month. Police personnel shall work a normal shift tour of eight hours and forty-five minutes, with a forty-five minute lunch period, except that administrative personnel may be required to work a nine hour tour with a one hour lunch period.

Holidays

All city employees are entitled to . . . . . . holidays per year, and if the holiday falls on Sunday, the following Monday shall be observed. In addition, other holidays as proclaimed by the President of the United States or the Governor of the state will also be observed.

Uniformed personnel required to work holidays shall . . . .

. . . . .²
(conditions.)

Vacations

All city employees are entitled to . . . . . . working days vacation per year. After . . . . . . years, the period increases to . . . . . . work-

---

² Complete conditions.

ing days, and after ...... years, to ...... working days. No person shall accumulate more than ...... working days vacation. Vacations shall be arranged for the convenience of the department, but employees' preference will be given every consideration. Normally, vacations will be scheduled between May 1 and September 30 of each year.

Sick Leave

Sick leave shall be accrued at the rate of ...... day(s) per month worked, and may be accrued from year to year to a ...... days limit. It may be used to cover absences from duty for only those reasons specified in the rules and regulations. A doctor's certificate is required for absences of more than five days.

Retirement System[3]

The city is under .... retirement system inaugurated in ...... and since then, all employees are covered by the act. Special sections of the act cover the fire and police personnel relative to death benefits and retirement age. Deductions are made on an actuarial basis from the salaries of all employees after a minimum of .... service, and it is credited to their account in the retirement fund.

(date)

Medical Plan

On ...., the city made available to employees the .... health plan. An employee may elect to participate in the plan, and coverage for the employee's family is also provided. Regular deductions to cover the premiums are made from the employee's salary.

(date)

Pay Periods

Pay checks are distributed .... All deductions are itemized on the stub attached to each check.

(date(s))

---

[3] If police and fire personnel are covered by special retirement plan, so indicate.

APPENDIX C

GENERAL AND SPECIAL ORDERS

Orders are normally of two types, "General" and "Special," and are the means by which actions are directed or decisions announced. Orders may be written or verbal. Verbal orders of any significance should be confirmed in writing as soon as possible.

General Orders: General orders direct or announce official acts of permanent duration and general application, applying to all or a large part of the organization. This type of order usually becomes incorporated in a manual.

Special Orders: Special orders are issued to appoint, assign, promote, retire, demote, separate, direct, and/or authorize leave of absence, assign duties, assign badges or serial numbers, and to effect transfers.[1]

It is not difficult to see that orders serve a great number of purposes. This prevents making a specific statement that the examples cited above are the sole purposes and reasons for orders. It will probably be discovered that in the operation of an individual police department some variation may be necessary from the guides as set forth. This is normal and you must keep your selected objective in sight when adopting these means to your own program.

In the course of management and the issuance of routine orders, you will find occasions where orders already issued are not appropriate for some reason. What to do? Briefly the following actions will prevail as a general guide.

Revocation

Revoke when the original order has been determined void and

---

[1] Note that both types of orders may be utilized for procedural or operational matters; dependent on the scope of the subject.

without effect from its inception, and no action has been taken on the authority contained therein.

Rescission

Rescind only when you desire to keep the order in effect until a date specified therein or under conditions when some action has been taken.

Amendment

Amend when it is necessary to change the content of the original order or correct errors such as wrong badge numbers, etc.

Orders should be written clearly in "basic" English. Relax and write as you talk, keeping in mind the following points:

1. Complete—does it answer the question?
2. Concise—does it have extra verbage that confuses the issue?
3. Clear—will the *recipient* understand it?
4. Correct—is it accurate, has it been co-ordinated and is it compatible with policy?
5. Tenor right?—are you writing down or up to anyone, sarcastic, vulgar or impertinent?
6. Abbreviations—are all abbreviations standardized in the department?
7. Is it effective?—if you received the order could you understand, and, as important, comply?

MECHANICS INVOLVED

In writing orders we have discussed the purpose, what actions are covered, and how to write clearly. Now let us examine, briefly, the mechanics involved.

The simplicity with which we can generate a maze of paper work is magnificent. More interesting, and difficult, is the approach to preventing this proliferation of paper. Luther Gulick is credited with calling this the "Carboniferous and Neolithographic Age." Orders are an extension of authority and therefore must be a controlled factor of management. The following ideas are worthy of attention in this area:

1. Authority to compose an order should be vested in a single

organizational segment where possible. This may be the adjutant or executive. All other personnel who require orders to be published should request them from this section or individual.

2. The order should be researched for the following information:

    a. No similar order has been issued in the past.
    b. It is not in conflict with policy, law or present orders.
    c. The order is necessary.
    d. It will serve a real purpose in the organization.

3. The order should be drafted within the section responsible for publication. It may be necessary in a smaller department to call on others for help in this matter. (See Example 1 for the format of this draft.)

4. The order should be coordinated by all interested sections. They should be allowed to comment freely on the virtues or faults of the order. (See Example 5 for self-explanatory system of draft and coordination.)

5. Once these steps are completed and the differences resolved the order is published, distributed, and checked for compliance. At this point the decision as to whether it will be a general or special order will have been made. The scope is usually the determinant factor.

If it is to be a procedural matter two distributions are recommended. One as a general statement of procedure (see Example 2) for inclusion or as an amendment to the "Manual." The second for distribution to all concerned; this copy will include more elaborate details as well as a statement of purpose. This will help sell the order to the recipient. (See Example 3.) If only one step is desired it is recommended that Example 3 be used, especially in the early stages of organization and in the formation of a "Manual." As soon as enough orders are generated a manual nucleus is present, and may be expanded in any of the various methods as may be desired.

6. Finally, if there are numerous personnel actions they should be combined and published on a regular date such as the first of each month. (See Example 4.)

GENERAL (SPECIAL) ORDER NUMBER 21-68[1]

SUBJECT: BOOKING OF MISDEMEANOR OFFENDERS
PROPOSED EFFECTIVE DATE: July 25, 1968
PURPOSE: This order informs officers of the procedure and defines responsibilities for handling of misdemeanor offenders when being booked at
receiving stations.
PROCEDURE: Upon apprehension and arrival at a receiving station the officer
in charge of the receiving desk will . . . ., etc.

Signed . . . .
Chief of Police

---

[1] Numbering is optional. Here the number 21 indicates the twenty-first order
of the current year, the sixty-eighth year. This provides good continuity as well as
easy recall and reference.

Example 1

— — — —

OFFICE OF THE CHIEF OF POLICE

SPECIAL ORDER NUMBER 21-68   July 25, 1968
TO: All Department Personnel.
SUBJECT: Booking of misdemeanor offenders.
EFFECTIVE: July 25, 1968.
PROCEDURE: The following order constitutes an amendment to the Department Manual, Volume 2, Chapter 7, and all copies will be so amended
on or before the effective date.
2/7/10.05 Booking of misdemeanor offenders will be carried out by the
officer in charge as follows . . . ., etc.[1]

Signed . . . .
Chief of Police

---

[1] You will note that the number assigned this manual amendment is not related
to the order number. In this case we have used the standard decimal system, two
refers to Vol. 2, seven refers to Chapter 7, 10.05 refers to paragraph.

Example 2

OFFICE OF THE CHIEF OF POLICE

SPECIAL ORDER NUMBER 21-68   July 25, 1968
SUBJECT: Booking of misdemeanor offenders.
EFFECTIVE: July 25, 1968.
PURPOSE:[1] This order informs officers of the procedure and defines responsi-
    bilities for handling of misdemeanor offenders when being booked at
    receiving stations.
INFORMATION:[2] Municipal Code changes require that in the future . . . .
PROCEDURE:[3]
        I. The Officer . . . .[4]
        A. Under . . . .
            1. Under . . . .
                a) Under . . . .
                    (1) Under . . . .
                        (a) Under . . . .
                            i) Under . . . .
                            ii) Under . . . .
                                                Signed . . . .
                                                Chief of Police

_____

    [1] Under purpose we define, briefly, the purpose of the order when the order
concerns procedure. This will assist in the understanding and compliance by the
line pesonnel.
    [2] Any information on the background of the order may appear here. Things
such as legal requirements and code changes or matters that will enable the
user to better understand this order.
    [3] The procedure is as the name implies, a detailed explanation so there can be
no doubt as to what is proper.
    [4] The numbering system of itemization shown here demonstrates the standard
only and may be modified to suit your need.

Example 3

OFFICE OF THE CHIEF OF POLICE

SPECIAL ORDER NUMBER 22-68   July 31, 1968
SUBJECT: PERSONNEL ACTIONS, Month of July.
EFFECTIVE: August 1, 1968.
TO: ALL DIVISION COMMANDERS AND PERSONNEL CONCERNED.
     1. TRANSFERS:
         James S. Jones, Lieut. Pol. No. 764. From Detective to Traffic.
     2. PROMOTIONS:
         John J. Jack, Sgt. Pol. No. 894. From Sgt. to Lieut.
     3. RETIREMENTS:
         George P. Smith, Sgt. Pol. No. 999. Retired this date.
     4. TRAVEL:
         Sgt. Roger P. Jones, Pol. No. 222, is authorized to proceed to the city of Abstract, California, for the purpose of returning a fugitive. Travel will be performed by rail as expeditiously as possible. The officer is authorized to draw sufficient travel funds from the City Treasury under appropriation No. 775-59.

Signed . . . .
Chief of Police

Example 4

_____ _____ _____ _____

GENERAL (SPECIAL) ORDER DRAFT AND CONCURRENCE

Date: June 29, 1968

Date Received	*Title and Div.*[1]	*Concur*		*Signature*	*Date*
		Yes	*No*		
June 30	Chief of Det.	x		J. J. Doe	July 1
July 1	Traffic Division		x	W. J. Who	July 3

[1] In order to assure the desired distribution, the titles and divisions may be entered in this column by the drafting unit before it is placed in distribution.

_____ _____ _____ _____

NON-CONCURRENCE REPORT

COMMENT NO. 1   From: Chief Traffic Division   Date: July 3, 1968
     1. I do not concur with the proposed order for the following reasons:
         A. Paragraph 3 states " . . . ." This should read " . . . ."
         This revision allows the officer more room for discretion in the matter and would cause less difficulty in the implementation of the order.

W. J. Who
Lt. Traffic Division

Example 5

APPENDIX D

FEDERAL LAW ENFORCEMENT AGENCIES

I. DEPARTMENT OF DEFENSE

Department of the Army[1]

THE PROVOST MARSHAL GENERAL

The Provost Marshal General has staff responsibility for the broad functions of protective services, preserving law and order, and of crime prevention applicable Army-wide. He has staff responsibility for provost marshal and military police activities; criminal investigations and law enforcement; motor vehicle accident investigation, traffic control, and traffic law enforcement; apprehension of absentees; physical security; implementation of industrial defense activities; the Army Correction Program; and prisoners of war and civilian internees.

Department of the Air Force[2]

THE INSPECTOR GENERAL

The Inspector General acts as an adviser to the Chief of Staff and serves as a professional assistant to the Secretary of the Air Force. He determines the status of combat readiness, command mission accomplishment, logistic effectiveness and discipline; evaluates the efficiency, economy, and adequacy of the USAF; investigates matters within USAF jurisdiction involving crime, violations of public trust, subversion, disaffection, and related activities; directs the counterintelligence program; establishes security policy; develops and directs the ground, flight, missile and nuclear safety policies, programs and procedures; and estab-

---

[1] *United States Government Organization Manual* (Washington, D. C.: Government Printing Office), p. 157, 1967-68.

[2] *Ibid.*, p. 197.

lishes effective Air Force facilities for inspection, security, investigation, law enforcement, and safety.

Department of the Navy

The Department of the Navy does not maintain any official law enforcement units similar to the Departments of the Army and Air Force. Each Naval District and the Naval Commands provide their own law enforcement services through Shore Patrol units and Naval Intelligence offices.

II. DEPARTMENT OF HEALTH, EDUCATION, AND WELFARE

Children's Bureau

The Division of Juvenile Delinquency Services provides consultant service to police agencies through its consultant on Juvenile Control.

III. DEPARTMENT OF JUSTICE[3]

Federal Bureau of Investigation

The Director of the Federal Bureau of Investigation has charge of investigating all violations of Federal laws with the exception of those which have been assigned by legislative enactment or otherwise to some other Federal agency. The FBI has jurisdiction over some 170 investigative matters. Among the more important of these are espionage, sabotage, treason, and other subversive activities; kidnapping; extortion; bank robbery, burglary, and larceny; crimes on Government or Indian reservations; thefts of Government property; the Fugitive Felon Act; interstate transportation or transmission of wagering information, gambling devices or paraphernalia; interstate travel in aid of racketeering; fraud against the Government; election law violations; civil rights matters; and assaulting or killing the President or a Federal officer.

Counterfeiting, postal, customs, and internal revenue violations and illegal traffic in narcotic drugs are crimes handled by other Federal agencies.

---

[3] *Ibid.*, p. 225.

Immigration and Naturalization Service

Pursuant to Reorganization Plan V, approved June 4, 1940, and effective June 14, 1940, the Immigration and Naturalization Service was transferred from the Department of Labor to the Department of Justice.

The Immigration and Naturalization Service, created by the act of March 3, 1891 (26 Stat. 1085), administers the immigration and naturalization laws relating to the admission, exclusion, and deportation of aliens, and the naturalization of aliens lawfully resident in the United States. It investigates alleged violations of those laws and makes recommendations for prosecutions when deemed advisable. It patrols the borders of the United States to prevent the surreptitious entry of aliens into the United States in violation of law.

It supervises naturalization work in the specific courts designated by section 310 of the Immigration and Nationality Act (66 Stat. 239; 8 U.S.C. 1421) to have jurisdiction in such matters. This includes requirement of accountings from the clerks of such courts for naturalization fees collected, investigations—through field officers—of the qualifications of citizenship applicants, and representation of the Government at all court hearings. It cooperates with the public schools in providing citizenship textbooks and other services for the preparation of candidates for naturalization.

The Immigration and Naturalization Service also registers and fingerprints aliens in the United States as required by section 262 of the Immigration and Nationality Act (66 Stat. 224; 8 U.S.C. 1304).

IV. POST OFFICE DEPARTMENT[4]

Bureau of Postal Inspectors

The Chief Postal Inspector advises the Postmaster General, the Deputy Postmaster General, and other principal assistants on the condition and needs of the Service; directs the execution of policies, regulations, and procedures governing all investigations, in-

---

[4] *Ibid.*, 234.

cluding presentation of evidence to the Department of Justice and U. S. Attorneys in those of a criminal nature; directs operating inspections and audits, including comprehensive internal and contract auditing, for the Postal Service; and acts as Security Officer, Military Liaison Officer, and Defense Coordinator for the Postal Establishment.

He directs the selection, training, and supervision of inspection service personnel.

He maintains liaison with other investigative and law enforcement agencies, and administers payment of rewards for information and services.

V. DEPARTMENT OF STATE[5]

Office of Public Safety

Has primary responsibility for public safety programs; develops policies, standards, and programs in public safety assistance; coordinates public safety programs and operations with other appropriate agencies and AID offices; administers participant training in public safety; evaluates public safety activities; develops, recruits, and assigns AID public safety personnel.

VI. TREASURY DEPARTMENT[6]

Office of Special Assistant to the Secretary (for Enforcement)

This office was established by Treasury Department Order 147 (Rev. 2), dated August 10, 1965. The Special Assistant to the Secretary (for Enforcement) serves as the principal adviser to the Secretary on law enforcement matters and supervises the United States Secret Service, Bureau of Narcotics, Office of Law Enforcement Coordination, and the Treasury Enforcement School. In addition, he formulates law enforcement policies and programs for all Treasury enforcement activities, including those of the Bureau of Customs and Internal Revenue Service. Other functions of this office include cooperation on law enforcement matters with other Federal agencies, and with State and local governments,

---

[5] *Ibid.*, p. 93.
[6] *Ibid.*, pp. 97-127.

and serving as the United States representative with the International Criminal Police Organization (INTERPOL). He also supervises arrangements for mutual assistance between Treasury law enforcement agencies.

Bureau of Customs

Creation and Authority. The Bureau of Customs was created by the act of March 3, 1927 (44 Stat. 1381; 5 U.S.C. 281 [1964 Ed.]). Authority for the collection of customs revenue was established by the second, third, and fifth acts of the first Congress in 1789.

Purpose. The functions of the Bureau of Customs are: (1) to assess and collect duties and taxes on imported merchandise; (2) to control carriers and merchandise imported into or exported from the United States; and (3) to combat smuggling and frauds on the revenue and related functions.

Customs acts for and works closely with many other Federal agencies including the Department of Commerce in export control, collection of statistical data and related activities; the Patent and Copyright Offices in enforcement of copyright, trademark, and patent restrictions; the State Department in munitions control and the enforcement of neutrality laws; the Public Health Service; Immigration and Naturalization Service; Bureau of Narcotics; Food and Drug Administration; and other enforcement and investigative agencies.

INTERNAL REVENUE SERVICE

The Intelligence Division[7]

"The Intelligence Division of Internal Revenue Service is the enforcement arm of that service for criminal violations of the Internal Revenue Code except for those offenses involving narcotics, liquor, tobacco, and firearms.

---

[7] Earl MacPherson, *A Survey of the Development, Organization, and Activities of the Investigative Law Enforcement Agencies of the United States Treasury Department,* John W. Donner Publication No. 5, School of Public Administration, University of Southern California, Los Angeles, 1958. (See also *U.S. Government Organization Manual,* Internal Revenue Service.)

"In the enforcement of these laws, Special Agents of Intelligence Division emphasize investigations involving racketeers, gamblers, and other criminals and undesirables.

"Special Agents also investigate applicants for enrollment to practice before the Treasury Department, and such other duties as may be assigned by the Secretary of the Treasury or the Commissioner of Internal Revenue.

"Income Tax Frauds: Most discrepancies in income tax payments are investigated and handled as civil affairs by Internal Revenue Agents and clerical personnel within a District Director's office. In general, the investigation is referred to Intelligence only when the person involved is of the criminal element or the taxes lost are of such a sum as to warrant the possibility of criminal prosecution.

"Wagering Tax Investigations: A few years ago Congress passed a law requiring a federal occupational tax to be paid for accepting wagers. This law was passed, not to obtain revenue but, to aid state, county, and local law enforcement agencies who had recommended legislation of this type in order that the resources of the federal government would be of greater assistance to these other law enforcement agencies in eliminating rackteering. The Intelligence Division is charged with enforcing this law."

Enforcement Branch of the Alcohol and Tobacco Tax Division[8]

"Some of the primary activities of the Alcohol and Tobacco Tax Division include the suppression of the non-taxpaid liquor and tobacco traffic, which involves the detection of violations, apprehension of offenders, the seizure of contraband, and means and instruments used in the commission of crimes, and the securing and reporting of evidence sufficient to sustain convictions. The ultimate objective of the enforcement program is the protection of the revenue.

"In addition, the Secretary of the Treasury has assigned certain other duties to this unit. Among them are the curbing of the

---

[8] *Ibid.*, pp. 81, 83, 85.

liquor traffic into dry states under the provisions of the Twenty-First Amendment to the Constitution . . . , the regulation of the liquor industry as a whole and the suppression of violations within the industry; the collection of certain federal occupational taxes, and the enforcement of the National and the Federal Firearms Acts.

"The Liquor Traffic: Specifically the liquor laws of the United States deal with the manufacture, importation, exportation, stamping, packaging, storing, removal, and concealment of alcoholic beverages. Most of the violations of these liquor laws occur in connection with the operation of illicit distilleries.

"The National Firearms Act: Another major activity of Alcohol and Tobacco Tax involves the investigation of possible violations of the National Firearms Act, the federal tax law which pertains to the manufacture, sale, importation, transportation, registration, transfer, and possession of such lethal weapons as machine guns, machine pistols, sawed-off rifles and shotguns, silencers, fountain pen pistols, and other weapons of this type. It becomes apparent upon study of the tax rate scheduled by this law that the taxes imposed under this act are not meant to obtain revenue but rather as a regulatory measure.

"The Federal Firearms Act: The Federal Firearms Act, which tended to utilize Congress' power to regulate interstate and foreign commerce was passed into law on June 30, 1938. This law, not a taxing measure, provided that the interstate transportation of any firearm was subject to federal regulation, and prohibited the interstate transportation of firearms by ex-convicts who had previously been convicted of certain crimes."

Internal Security Division[9]

"The jurisdiction of the Internal Security Division of Internal Revenue Service is more that of an internal affairs agency, rather more than a more general law enforcement unit.

"Investigations generally conducted by Internal Security Division inspectors are of two broad types. The first involves conduct and character investigations of prospective employees of the

---

[9] *Ibid.*, pp. 85-87.

Internal Revenue Service and certain other agencies of the Treasury Department and is often called a background investigation.

"The second type of investigation made by inspectors involves improper, illegal, or unauthorized activities of Internal Revenue Service Employees. The Internal Security Division also makes investigations for other agencies within the Treasury Department but outside of the Internal Revenue Service, at the request of the agency staff. For instance, an inspector may be assigned to investigate an alleged illegal act committed by a Narcotics Agent, a Customs Agent, or a Secret Service Agent, if the particular agency head requests assistance from Inspection Service.

"Investigations are often conducted jointly with the Secret Service, Customs, the FBI, Intelligence, Post Office Inspectors, Narcotics, and other federal investigative agencies.

"Reports compiled by Inspectors and forwarded to responsible administrative officers, in cases involving alleged misconduct of federal employees, do not carry recommendations, opinions, or conclusions. These reports are merely factual statements as developed by the Inspectors.

"Other Investigations Conducted by the Internal Security Division: All tort claims involving, and filed against, Internal Revenue Service employees on official duty are investigated by Inspectors, as are charges of a discriminatory promotion or discharge policy, allegedly being pursued by officials of any Internal Revenue Service office or division.

"On occasion, Inspectors discover violations of state or local laws which are referred to the responsible agency for further action."

Bureau of Narcotics[10]   *Dept of Justice*

The Bureau of Narcotics was created under the Treasury Department by an act of Congress, June 14, 1930 (46 Stat. 585; U.S.C. 282–282a (1964 Ed.)) The law provides that the Commissioner of Narcotics, appointed by the President, shall direct activities of the Bureau as prescribed by the Secretary or required by law.

---

[10] *Loc. cit.* (U. S. Government Manual), p. 123.

Administration of Laws. The Bureau of Narcotics, under the Commissioner, supervises the administration of sections of the Internal Revenue Code, the Opium Poppy Control Act of 1942, and other statutes related to narcotic drugs and marihuana. The Bureau also administers the permissive features of the Narcotic Drugs Import and Export Act. The Bureau of Narcotics determines the quantities of crude opium and coca leaves to be imported into the United States for medical and scientific use. It also issues permits for import of the two crude drugs and for export of drugs and preparations manufactured under United States laws and regulations.

Under the Narcotics Manufacturing Act of 1960, the Bureau of Narcotics is responsible for limiting the manufacture of natural and synthetic narcotic drugs exclusively for medical and scientific purposes by administering a system of licenses and quotas for manufacturers. Consistent with this country's treaty obligations, if needed to meet domestic medical and scientific requirements, under the Opium Poppy Control Act of 1942, the Bureau may issue licenses for production of opium poppies and for manufacture of opium products.

Enforcement. The Bureau of Narcotics is responsible for detection, investigation, and prevention of violations of Federal narcotic and marihuana laws and related statutes. It also cooperates with the Bureau of Customs in enforcing the prohibitive features of the Narcotic Drugs Import and Export Act.

Cooperation With Foreign Countries and States. The Bureau joins with the Department of State to fulfill the United States international obligations concerning traffic in narcotics. It also cooperates with the various States to suppress the abuse of narcotic drugs and marihuana; operates a narcotic law enforcement training program for local and State police officers; and maintains statistical data on the extent of narcotic drug addiction in the United States.

United States Secret Service[11]

The responsibilities and jurisdiction of the United States Secret Service are prescribed by law in title 18, U. S. Code, section 3056.

---

[11] *Ibid.*

Subject to the direction of the Secretary of the Treasury, the United States Secret Service is authorized to protect the person of the President of the United States, the members of his immediate family, the President-elect, the Vice President or other officer next in the order of succession to the Office of President, and the Vice President-elect; protect the person of a former President and his wife during his lifetime and the person of a widow and minor children of a former President for a period of 4 years after he leaves or dies in office, unless such protection is declined.

The Secret Service is also authorized to detect and arrest any person committing any offense against the laws of the United States relating to coins, obligations, and securities of the United States and of foreign governments; detect and arrest any person violating any of the provisions of sections 508, 509, and 871 of title 18 of the U. S. Code; execute warrants issued under the authority of the United States; carry firearms; offer and pay rewards for services or information looking toward the apprehension of criminals; and perform such other functions and duties as are authorized by law.

In the performance of their duties under section 3056, title 18, U. S. Code, agents of the Secret Service are authorized to make arrests without warrant for any offense against the United States committed in their presence, or for any felony cognizable under the laws of the United States if they have reasonable grounds to believe that the person to be arrested has committed or is committing such felony.

The Director of the Secret Service is charged with the supervision of the White House police force and the Treasury guard force. The White House police force protects the White House, Executive offices, and grounds, and the President and his immediate family. The Treasury guard force is responsible for the safety of many billions of dollars in currency, bonds, and other securities in the Treasury Building and its vaults.

Information on the Secret Service can be obtained by contacting any District Office or the Secret Service Headquarters, Office of the Assistant to the Director, Information and Liaison.

REPOSSESSIONS

Officers are sometimes called to the scene of a dispute which has arisen over the attempt of a person to repossess a vehicle or some other type of property. Occasionally, criminal acts are committed by the disputing persons. In such cases, the officer may need to make an immediate arrest if the offense is committed in his presence. It may be necessary for him to advise the disputing persons about private persons' arrest procedure, or refer the parties to the prosecuting attorney for advice on criminal prosecution.

This brief discussion of the basic rights of buyers and sellers and the description of a few of the restrictions on repossessions is intended only to make the officer aware of the types of situations he may encounter in repossession disputes. The officer *must not* give advice on civil matters, and he *must* confine his activities to keeping the peace.

Conditional Sales Contracts

The history of conditional sales contracts, used in most installment plan buying, dates back about fifty years. The old style contracts were often full of loopholes which permitted the buyer to void the contract. Every time a loophole was discovered, subsequent contracts were written to eliminate it. As a result, today's contracts are usually binding.

When a person buys property on time he usually signs a conditional sales contract. This contract contains the conditions of the sale to which both the seller and the buyer agree. The conditions usually are printed in small type, and the buyers frequently neglect to read them carefully. The conditions of sales contracts vary with the company, but there are certain provisions common to most of them. In almost all cases, the title of ownership rests with the seller until the final payment is made. The buyer may be in possession of the merchandise, but he does not own it until it is fully paid for. Another condition provides that the seller may recover his property if the buyer becomes delinquent in payments. This is the part of the contract which causes the most trouble.

Who Can Repossess

The right of the seller to repossess is generally accepted. Altogether, however, there are three groups of persons who can repossess property. The first group includes the seller and his employees. The employees must work for the seller on a full time basis, and not have been hired just for a special or temporary job. People in this group need not have a state license.

The second group includes the seller's "successor in interest," and the employees of the "successor in interest." A successor in interest is one who buys the contract from the seller. For example, the original seller turns the sales contract over to a bank, to let the bank finance the sale. The bank would become the successor in interest, and its full time employees may repossess without a state license.

The third group includes licensed collection agencies. A collection agency operates by soliciting accounts or recovering property for a seller. To prevent irresponsible persons from attempting to repossess, a collection agency must have a state license, and is regulated by the state.

Method of Repossession

When a buyer becomes delinquent in his payments, the repossessor may attempt to recover the property. There are, however, definite limits to what a repossessor can do in his attempt to repossess. The repossession must be made in a peaceful manner; the repossessor must not commit an assault or battery, and he must not cause a disturbance.

Reporting Missing Property

Repossession of merchandise sometimes results in the buyer's attempting to report the property as stolen. This is particularly true in the case of automobiles. For this reason, most departments require that any person who wishes to make a stolen car report be asked if the car was purchased on a conditional sales contract, and whether the buyer is behind in his payments. Vehicle records should be checked before submitting stolen auto reports to be teletyped. Repossessors are required to report the repossession of an automobile, and checking with vehicle records usually prevents the taking of an unnecessary stolen car report.

Repossessor's Rights

An authorized repossessor may recover property anywhere he can find it, provided he does not break and enter an enclosure to effect the repossession. He does not need the permission of the buyer because the buyer is not the legal owner of the property. The repossessor may even go upon the private property of the buyer for this purpose. For example, a repossessor may repossess an automobile parked in a driveway, or porch furniture on the porch of the buyer's home. However, the repossessor cannot enter a house to recover property without permission from the occupant, and he cannot break into a locked garage to repossess (without a court order).

Buyer's Right

The general rule is that property in the possession of the buyer cannot be physically taken from him against his express objections. Where the buyer of property upon conditional sales defaults in his payments, and by the terms of the agreement the seller is authorized in such event to retake the property, the seller is entitled under this power to repossess the property if he can do so peaceably; but, if the buyer objects and protests against the seller's retaking the property, and obstructs him in so doing, it is the duty of the seller to resort to legal process to enforce his rights to repossession. The repossessor is not entitled to use force, and he is guilty of an assault and battery or of disturbing the peace, as the case may be, if he does.

Repossessor in Possession of Property

Once the repossession of property is complete, the repossessor is entitled to retain possession against the objections of the buyer or anyone else. For example, while no one else is present, a repossessor gains possession of a car parked in a driveway or in front of a house. He drives the car out of the driveway and proceeds down the street for half a block. The buyer pursues him, and finally succeeds in jumping into the car. At this point the repossession is complete, and the repossessor does not have to return the car to the buyer. As a general rule, repossession is complete if the buyer has to pursue the repossessor and the property in order to object to the repossession.

Third Person in Possession

When property is in the possession of any person, regardless of his connection with the buyer, the repossessor has no right to take it against the person's objection. For example, the buyer has loaned a vehicle to a friend. While the friend is in the car, or while the car is in the friend's locked garage, the repossessor has no right to take the car. In such case, the buyer's rights are transferred to the person who possesses the property with the buyer's consent. If, however, the friend left the loaned vehicle parked on the street while he shopped, he could not be considered in possession, and the repossessor could take the car. A friend or neighbor of the buyer has no right to object to repossession of property unless that person has actual possession of the property with the consent of the buyer. For example, the repossessor prepares to take a car from in front of the buyer's home. The buyer is away at the time, but a neighbor objects to the repossession. In this case, the repossessor has a right to take the property.

If the car is left in a commercial parking lot or garage, the repossessor has no right to take it from the parking lot or garage attendant who has been specifically charged with responsibility for the property.

Settling Disputes

At the scene of a repossession, the officer should first inquire about the repossessor's right to take the property. Repossessors usually have some identification—a copy of the contract, a company identification card, or a description of the property along with an authorization from the seller to repossess it.

When the officer is satisfied that the repossessor is not a thief, it should be determined whether the other person involved is the actual buyer, or a third person legally in possession of the property and thus entitled to assert the buyer's right to resist possession. If so, he should be asked if he objects to the repossession of the property. The repossessor has no right to repossess over the objection of a qualified person in possession.

When a proper objection is raised, which will not permit the repossession, the repossessor must resort to legal action. Most legitimate repossessors are familiar with their limitations, but their job is to complete the recovery of the property. They may use stealth, trick, or bluff, or any other peaceful procedure to repossess, but they usually try to avoid causing trouble. Trouble is more likely to be caused by unlicensed or unauthorized persons attempting to repossess property.

Advising Involved Parties

The best advice an officer can give persons involved in a dispute over repossession is to direct them to see their attorneys. The repossessor should be reminded that he is obligated to make the property recovery in a peaceful manner, and, if it cannot be accomplished peacefully, he must resort to legal processes.

Avoiding Repossession

A licensed repossessor went to the home of a buyer to attempt repossession of some property. The repossessor knocked on the door and a feminine voice inside the house asked who was at the door. He identified himself and stated his business. The woman's voice then asked him to wait a minute. He stood on the front porch and smoked a cigarette; after finishing it he knocked once more. Again the woman asked him to wait. A minute later, a Sheriff's car stopped in front of the house, and the woman, dressed in a flimsy robe, opened the front door and shouted "Rape." The repossessor had to talk fast to convince the deputies of his legitimate purpose at the house. The tactics used by this woman illustrate the length to which buyers may go to avoid repossession.

Commission of a Crime

If either the repossessor or the buyer of the property claims a crime has been committed, and immediate action is unnecessary, the officer should take a crime report.

If immediate action is necessary, the officer must consider the rights of each party in determining whether or not a crime has been committed. If a buyer is advised of a repossessor's identity, and reason for his presence on private property, and then strikes the repossessor without provocation, the buyer has committed a battery. On the other hand, the repossessor may have committed an assault or battery if he attempts to take the property against the physical objection of the buyer.

Officers at the scene should, insofar as possible, confine their activities to keeping the peace. They may make an immediate arrest if a crime is committed in their presence and the public peace and safety is likely to be further endangered if no arrest is made. If a crime was committed before the officers arrived at the scene, or not in the presence of the officers, they may advise the parties on private persons' arrest procedure. Should the dispute reach the point where both parties become loud and quarrelsome, they should be advised that they may be committing a breach of the peace, for which violation both may be arrested.

Personal Property in Vehicle

The buyer of an automobile has the right to remove from the car any personal property or belongings, such as a suitcase, clothing, a camera, etc., before the repossessor takes the vehicle. The buyer does not have the right to remove anything that is attached to the car (spotlights, radio, heater, etc.), even though the buyer purchased the equipment and attached it after obtaining the vehicle from the seller. The repossessor will, however, give the buyer a receipt for such equipment or accessories and the buyer may regain them from the seller after the car has been repossessed.

If a vehicle containing personal property is repossessed without the buyer's knowledge, he may attempt to make a report of theft of personal property. However, the seller or his successor in interest is responsible to the buyer for any personal property taken with the vehicle at the time of the repossession. An officer should not take a theft report if he is informed that the vehicle might have been repossessed, but should refer the citizen to the repossessor.

Legal Procedure for Repossession

When the seller fails to recover his property by peaceful methods, he may go to court and file a "Claim and Delivery" action. He must then post a bond. The court issues a Writ of Replevin, which is served by an officer of the court—usually the Marshal. Court officers operate under court order, and are entitled to use any necessary force in executing the particular writ. Occasionally, radio car officers are called to assist a court officer attempting to serve a Writ of Replevin of "Claim and Delivery." The officers should give only that assistance necessary to prevent the commission of a crime.

INDEX